Taxation and
Economic Development
in Tropical Africa

JOHN F. DUE

THE M.I.T. PRESS

MASSACHUSETTS INSTITUTE OF TECHNOLOGY

CAMBRIDGE, MASSACHUSETTS, 1963

LIBRARY OF CONGRESS CATALOG CARD NUMBER: 63-22437

Printed in the United States of America

*To my wife Jean
and my sister Shirley*

Preface

THIS VOLUME is based on a series of lectures given by the author during the week of December 3–7, 1962, at Cambridge, under the auspices of the Harvard Law School International Program in Taxation and the M.I.T. School of Industrial Management. These lectures, in turn, were developed from a study of taxation in eight African countries with British background, undertaken during the spring of 1962 while the author was on sabbatical leave from the University of Illinois. Field work on the study included interviews with officials of the Ministries of Finance, Local Government, and Economic Development of the various countries, persons in charge of tax administration at various levels of government, and others familiar with the tax systems. Portions of the material presented in the lectures have been rewritten to lessen duplication and to elaborate on certain sections.

I am greatly indebted to the officials of the governments of the eight countries covered, including those of the regional governments of Nigeria, the territorial governments of Rhodesia, and the East Africa Common Services Organization, for their assistance, without which the study would have been impossible. I should also like to express appreciation to the African Studies Program of the Social Science Research Council for travel assistance provided and to Professor Oliver Oldman of the Harvard Law School and Professors J. Daniel Nyhart and Carroll L. Wilson of M.I.T. for the invitation to give the lectures on which this monograph is based. And last but not least, I should like to express appreciation to my wife Jean for her invaluable assistance in planning and executing the project, and to my sister Shirley for so capably looking after all problems in Champaign–Urbana while we were away and maintaining communications with us while we were traveling in Africa.

JOHN F. DUE

Urbana, Illinois   August 1, 1963

Contents

1. The Eight Tropical African Countries
   of British Background   *1*

2. The Tax Structures   *25*

3. Income Taxation: Structure   *31*

4. Income Taxation: Staff and Operations   *51*

5. The Personal Tax   *61*

6. Customs, Excise, and Export Duties   *83*

7. Taxation of Real Property   *102*

8. Financing Federation   *119*

9. Tax Policy and Economic Development   *144*

Index   *167*

Taxation and
Economic Development
in Tropical Africa

1 The Eight Tropical African Countries

of British Background[1]

THE YEARS since the end of World War II have witnessed a phenomenal increase in the interest in economic and political development of the underdeveloped areas of the world, and in the efforts of these countries to speed such development. The trend has coincided with the virtual disappearance of colonialism, but is by no means confined to the countries which have recently become independent. In Latin America, in Asia, in Africa, the overriding goal has become that of economic growth, with the specific aim of bringing the per capita real income in a short period of time from very low levels to those of the highly developed countries of Western Europe and North America.

It is widely accepted in these countries that governments must play a major role in spurring economic growth; the slow growth in the past is taken as evidence that government participation is imperative. Likewise, it is recognized that the tax systems employed to finance government activities may have very substantial influence, for good or bad, upon the rate and pattern of growth. As a consequence, substantial attention has been given to tax systems and their possible reform in light of requirements of economic

[1] Portions of the material in this chapter appeared in the article entitled "Some Observations on Economic and Political Development in Tropical Africa," in the August, 1962, issue of the *Quarterly Review of Economics and Business*, and are used by permission of the *Review*.

growth. For example, there have been two major conferences in Latin America in the last two years on the subject, as well as more intensive study of the tax systems of particular countries. While the tax systems of some African countries have been subjected to detailed study, there has been less general review, and little information on African experience is available, particularly in the United States. Accordingly, this study was devoted to an analysis of the tax structures of the eight countries of tropical Africa that are, or have been, British colonies or protectorates. Attention was given to the tax systems and administration in light of the general economic, political, and educational background, to tax policies designed specifically to aid economic growth, and to the significance that the experience may offer for tax policy in other underdeveloped areas. Chapter 1 presents a general survey of the eight countries, with particular reference to questions of economic development; Chapters 2 through 7 review the tax structures by type of tax; and Chapter 8 deals with the special problems of taxation in the federal areas. The final chapter provides a broader review of the general question of taxation and economic development in light of the African experience.

THE EIGHT COUNTRIES

Table 1.1 presents a brief summary of the major statistics of the countries.[2] Both population and gross national product figures are in large measure estimates; with a high percentage of the population dependent largely on subsistence agriculture, it is impossible to develop entirely satisfactory figures. The currencies of all of the countries are maintained at par with the English pound sterling, and thus the figures given are comparable. The four East African countries, plus Aden, use a common currency, issued by the East Africa Currency Board. Throughout this study the reference to pounds will be to those of the respective countries.[3]

The three West African countries, Sierra Leone, Ghana, and Nigeria, vary greatly in population. Nigeria is the largest country in Africa, with nearly twice the population of the second largest (Egypt). British domination gradually spread northward from the coastal areas, and not until 1903 was the entire area subject to

[2] The other British countries of tropical Africa, which are not included in the study, are Gambia, on the west coast, with a population of 300,000, and the three High Commission territories, Bechuanaland, Swaziland, and Basutoland, the last two named being almost entirely surrounded by the Republic of South Africa.

[3] We shall use *s.* as the abbreviation for shilling, and / to separate shillings and pence. The East African shilling contains 100 cents instead of 12 pence; shillings and cents are separated by a decimal point.

2

TABLE 1.1   MAJOR FEATURES OF THE COUNTRIES, 1960

Country	Estimated Population (millions)	Gross Domestic Product at Factor Prices (millions of pounds)†	Gross Domestic Product, per Capita (pounds)	Independence Gained
Sierra Leone	2.5	n.a.	n.a.	1961
Ghana	6.7	560‡	84	1957
Nigeria	37	1100§	30	1960
Kenya	6.5*	222	34	scheduled for December, 1963
Uganda	6.5	152	23	1962 (October)
Tanganyika	9	185	21	1961
Zanzibar	0.3	12	40	scheduled for December, 1963
Federation of Rhodesia and Nyasaland	8.5*	557	66	**

* Of these, about 40,000 in Kenya and 300,000 in Rhodesia are Europeans. The numbers of Europeans in the other countries are much smaller.

† The currencies of all of these countries are maintained at par with the British pound sterling. The four East African countries use a common currency (together with Aden).

‡ At market prices.

§ Estimated; 1957 figure, £910.

** Federation to be dissolved December 31, 1963. Northern Rhodesia and Nyasaland to become independent shortly; future status of Southern Rhodesia in doubt.

British control. Independence was granted in 1960 after several years of negotiations, with a federal structure (described in Chapter 8) designed to provide sufficient autonomy to the three regions to hold the country together as a unit, despite great diversities of tribal groups, religions, economic interests, and other considerations. The country has thus far been highly successful in maintaining a stable democratic government, based on a compromise between the principal party of the conservative and less developed north and that of the more liberal eastern region. The general economic policy of the country has been a relatively conservative one as well, with greater stress on private enterprise and less on governmental participation than in Ghana. The regions of Nigeria will be described more fully in Chapter 8.

Ghana, called the Gold Coast prior to independence, with about six and a half million people, has the most highly developed African culture and economy in all of tropical Africa. The per capita income is nearly three times that of Nigeria. Ghana has moved much

3

further than any of the other countries toward Africanization of the civil service; in most fields, expatriates are used only as advisers. The economy is heavily dependent on cocoa, of which Ghana is one of the world's major producers. Thus the economy is very sensitive to changes in world cocoa prices, and declines in recent years have created major problems. Ghana was the first of the tropical African countries to gain independence (1957). The country had come under complete British domination only after 1900. The six years since independence have been marked by considerable departure from democracy, by development of an essentially one-party state, and by some use of the technique of imprisoning political opponents. However, the government has pushed development programs vigorously, and while some of the programs and policies may

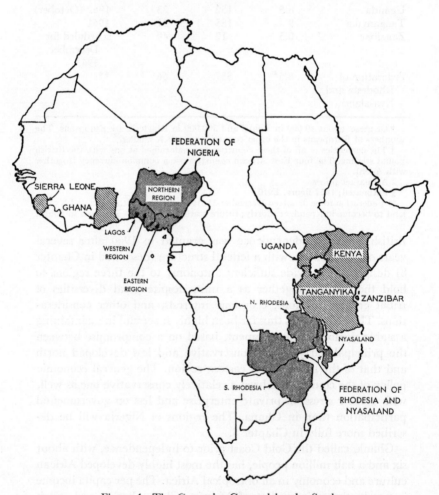

Figure 1. The Countries Covered by the Study

be questioned, the sense of drive and initiative and dedication to a goal is very strong. Although Ghana has made use of aid, technical and financial, from Eastern Europe as well as Western, it is in no sense a Communist country.

The third West African country, Sierra Leone, is by far the smallest, with two and a half million people, and except for the capital, Freetown, the least developed. Freetown, which has one of the finest harbors in the world, became a British colony in 1808, but control was extended over the remainder of the country very slowly, being completed only in 1896. Though Freetown is a modern city, the remainder of the country is relatively primitive, with limited educational facilities and poor transportation. The country has relatively poor resources. Diamonds and iron ore are the chief sources of foreign exchange. There is only very limited manufacturing.

The West African countries have no non-African settler element of any magnitude. Climatic and health conditions for decades did not favor white settlement, and ultimately policies which barred non-African landownership were established. Europeans came on a temporary basis in business and in government jobs, and except for Lebanese merchants, who typically did not settle permanently, there were few other non-Africans. Thus the racial tensions of East Africa have been avoided, and there has been greater entry on the part of Africans into trade and industrial employment.

British East Africa consisted originally of the two mainland countries of Uganda and Kenya, plus the island of Zanzibar; after World War I the former German East African colony of Tanganyika came under British jurisdiction. The three mainland countries are described in greater detail in Chapter 8. Uganda, long ruled on an indirect basis in the fashion of Northern Nigeria, with substantial power left in the hands of the local hereditary rulers, is the most strictly "African" of these countries, and in this respect resembles West Africa. It is a major producer of coffee and cotton. Independence was gained peacefully in October, 1962, and in spite of some rivalries between the ancient kingdoms, Uganda offers promise of stable political and economic development. Tanganyika, with the lowest per capita income of any of the countries in the study, and with great transportation problems, became independent in 1961 under the guidance of one of the most competent of the African political leaders, Julius Nyerere. Neither Uganda nor Tanganyika has any significant white settler groups; both have some plantation agriculture, but of limited scope. Both have substantial Indian elements, particularly in trade and service occupations.

The third East African country, Kenya, is similar to its neighbors in some respects but with a substantial white settler element. This has been the source, on the one hand, of more rapid economic growth and higher per capita income but, on the other hand, of substantial racial tension, which reached its highest peak in the Mau Mau outbreaks of a decade ago. This problem, plus substantial tribal antagonism, has delayed independence, which is now scheduled for December 12, 1963. One of the two major parties represents the dominant Kikuyu and Luo tribes of central Kenya, the other the minor tribes. There is grave danger of outbreaks of violence, with some possibility of disintegration of the country as a unit. The fourth country, the tiny British Protectorate of Zanzibar, was long controlled by the Arabs; it was the major depot for East African trade in both commodities and slaves, and the city is the oldest major trade center in all East Africa. Nominally still ruled by the Sultan (whose ancestors ruled Oman, in Arabia), Zanzibar became a British protectorate in 1891. It is the world's principal producer of cloves. There is a sharp division between the dominant Arab group and the lower-income African group, and this clash delayed the granting of independence, now scheduled December 10, 1963.

The eighth country is the Federation of Rhodesia and Nyasaland, made up of the three formerly separate protectorates of Nyasaland, Northern Rhodesia, and Southern Rhodesia. The Federation was formed in 1953, but failed to bring unity of the European and African populations. As Nyasaland and Northern Rhodesia gained African governments, they insisted upon the dissolution of the Federation, which was controlled largely by the white settler groups of Southern Rhodesia. The dissolution was approved by Great Britain in 1963 and will become effective December 31, 1963. Nyasaland and Northern Rhodesia will shortly become independent; the future of Southern Rhodesia is by no means clear at the moment. The three constituent parts of Rhodesia are described more fully in Chapter 8. Southern Rhodesia has been self-governing since 1923, and the Federation enjoyed substantial autonomy and status almost like that of a dominion. Rhodesia is one of the world's principal producers of copper, and a major exporter of tobacco products.

The term "Rhodesia" will be used throughout to designate the Federation.

SOME COMMON FEATURES

The eight countries have a number of features in common. As noted, all have either become independent or, with one exception, are about to become independent in the near future. All are in relatively early stages of economic development in many respects, so far as the great majority of the people are concerned, with low per capita incomes, between £20 and £84 ($56 to $235, at current exchange rates). The economies are characterized by primitive hand-cultivation agriculture and very limited use of capital equipment. Yet virtually all persons have some contact with the market sector of the economy through sale of produce, part-time work, and purchase of manufactured goods; very few families are entirely self-sufficient. All of the countries produce substantial amounts of farm products for export. By contrast with the primitive agriculture and native villages, unchanged for centuries, are features comparable to those of the more developed economies—modern cities, buses, airlines, modern manufacturing plants, etc. West African cities are truly "African" cities, with some European features grafted on; the East and Central African cities are largely European-Indian creations; Uganda, for example, had no towns or cities when the British came, families living instead on their own isolated farms. In Kenya and the Rhodesias particularly, a highly developed European type of economy has been superimposed upon a primitive native economy, but thus far it has affected only relatively small segments of the population. In all countries the drive for economic growth is very strong, with the goal of bringing per capita incomes within a few years to the levels of those of Western Europe, and thus to attain in a few decades a development which took centuries in other parts of the world.

CONDITIONS FAVORING ECONOMIC DEVELOPMENT

These areas have certain advantages favoring economic development compared with many other relatively underdeveloped areas in the world; they also have certain unique difficulties and suffer others in common with all countries seeking to catch up rapidly in development. The advantages will be noted in this section and the difficulties in subsequent ones.

Population-Resources Relationships

Particularly as compared with Asia, the African countries have very favorable ratios of population to food supply. Although diets typically lack adequate protein, there is little basic deficiency in food output, even with present primitive methods of cultivation and continued use in some areas of the wasteful practice of shifting cultivation to newly burned areas in the jungle. As a consequence there is a much greater potential margin for production in excess of subsistence needs, which is of utmost importance for economic development and which is lacking in the overpopulated countries of the Far East. Improved medical care will, of course, increase the

7

rate of population growth. But the existing margin is very substantial. Only in limited areas, such as parts of Eastern Nigeria, is there any basic overpopulation.[4] Two reasons for this, incidentally, are the relatively high age of persons before "marriage" in one form or another takes place, and the relatively long intervals between successive babies.

Cultural Advantages

Although there are certain cultural factors in Africa which retard development, as will be noted in a later section, these appear to many observers to be less significant than in other areas, particularly Asia. One of the most significant characteristics of primitive societies is the dominance of tradition—the resistance to cultural change in all its forms. This is to be found in Africa as well as elsewhere. But from all indications, it appears to be less strong in Africa than in the cultures of much of Asia. There is greater willingness to accept change and to undertake new forms of economic activity.

British Traditions

Although some political leaders of African countries would be reluctant to admit the fact, without question the years of British colonial domination resulted in the implantation of various British traditions and institutions. Not all of these are necessarily advantageous (such as the color bar, the nondecimal currency system, and the emphasis on classical education in the universities, which is not well suited to modern Africa), and others were transferred only very slowly and imperfectly. But the fact remains that there were significant beneficial effects. These become particularly apparent if comparison is made between these British areas and Liberia or various Latin-American countries.

A major contribution is the development of traditions of democratic government, with carefully prepared constitutions. Another is an important tradition of relative honesty in government, business, and personal relationships. While "dashes" are traditional in West Africa to get various services performed, the fact remains that the over-all standards are much better than in many underdeveloped areas. Another contribution is the basic importance attached to efficiency in the performance of tasks, and the minimization of bureaucratic red tape in government (so common in southern Europe).

The high prestige of the civil service, with its emphasis upon career personnel and selection in terms of qualifications, was also

[4] As in Latin America, there has been a flow of population to some large cities in excess of jobs, with serious overcrowding and shortage of food for some families.

transmitted to Africa, where in general the philosophy in this field is much closer to that of Britain than to that of the United States. Similarly, the institution of the Royal Commission as a means of reviewing various problems and making recommendations and the tendency of governments to accept the recommendations reflect British influence. The parliamentary form of government is in itself an aid to governmental action necessary for development. Tax systems are basically British, and while perhaps not always best suited to African conditions, they do reflect centuries of attention in England to the question of the most acceptable forms of taxation.

Other Considerations

The respect for elders is very widespread; this may make for conservatism, but it aids stability and lessens the appeal of demagogues. There is a tendency for voters to elect members of the hereditary ruling families to the legislative bodies.

OBSTACLES AND PROBLEMS

Any society in the early stages of economic development must, of course, be faced with certain obstacles to economic growth; if these had not existed, the economies in Africa would long ago have attained a much higher stage of development.

Tribalism

One of the major obstacles to political stability and economic development is the feature commonly referred to as tribalism—the important role of the tribes relative to that of the national governments, with the consequent difficulty of obtaining unity of policy and the danger of disintegration of the whole governmental structure. The degree of tribalism varies; it is weak in Ghana, for example, where the power of the Ghana government is well established, and in Tanganyika, where the large number of small tribes prevents any of them from being a serious rival to the Tanganyika government. It is strong in Uganda, where the Kingdom of Buganda occupies a large portion of the country (about one third of the population, and the wealthy and well-developed areas). There are important tribal considerations in Nigeria.

Part of the difficulty stems from the fact that these countries are not natural entities in any sense; their boundaries are neither natural nor related to tribal demarcation. Instead, the countries were essentially created by drawing lines on maps as the colonial powers completed the division of Africa in the latter part of the nineteenth century. For example, Northern Nigeria bears no resemblance at all to the southern portion of the country, has no indigenous ties with it, and was not even a portion of Nigeria until 1914. Much of the population of Tanganyika might more logically be included in Uganda. The surprising feature is not that of disintegrative tendencies, but that countries of such recent and artificial creation have any unity at all.

The consequences of tribalism vary somewhat with the circumstances, but they are in general undesirable from the standpoint of development. Political parties frequently follow tribal lines, as they do in Kenya; governments may represent uneasy compromises of various tribal points of view, as is true to some extent in Nigeria; and the rights of minority tribes may be neglected. Buganda has threatened at times to withdraw from the rest of Uganda; growth of the remainder of the country would in this event be hampered seriously, as would that of Buganda itself, the very heart of the country. Tribal warfare, so common before the British came, is a real possibility in some instances; Buganda and neighboring Bunyoro may yet come to an armed clash over the so-called lost counties, taken by Buganda just before the British established a protectorate over the country, and claimed ever since by Bunyoro. All in all, tribalism is a destabilizing and potentially destructive force that could seriously impair progress.

Nationalism

Even though the new states may suffer from lack of internal cohesiveness, at the same time they have rapidly developed strong sentiments of nationalism, which, coupled with the fact that many of them are very small, can impede economic growth. Except for Nigeria, none of the countries has a population in excess of ten million. Given the relatively low incomes, the markets are too small to allow efficient conduct of most types of manufacturing, yet each country is determined to develop its own industry. In East Africa, fortunately, a common market was developed long before independence; the three major East African countries have a single external tariff (with minor exceptions) and no tariffs on shipments among the three countries. There is some danger, however, that the system may break down under the impact of independence and nationalism, particularly since Tanganyika, and to a lesser extent Uganda, have long believed that the common market favors Kenya at their expense. Federation of these countries would have important economic advantages and is once again the subject of serious consideration. In West Africa, physical separation makes closer cooperation difficult; there is some tendency for Ghana to associate itself more closely economically with its French-speaking neighbors than with Nigeria and Sierra Leone.

Considerations of nationalism also make more difficult the task of getting outside capital for economic development. There are strong sentiments against foreign domination of economic activity, which result in some restrictions on such investments. Even in the countries which are most sympathetic to outside investment, such as Nigeria, there are fears that possible political instability and the rise of extremist governments may ultimately endanger foreign investments.

On the other hand, of course, the spirit of nationalism tends to reduce the divisive influence of tribalism and to promote a spirit of progress which is advantageous to growth.

Prejudices

Racial prejudices constitute a major obstacle in the way of the optimum use of resources for economic growth. Some of these are a product of past policies imposed by the dominant European groups; partly they seem to be inevitable products of racial differences. Some of these prejudices are against other Africans, a result in part of the tribalism noted above. For example, Northern Nigeria, with fewer educated Africans than the south, once employed many persons from southern Nigeria in clerical and other posts. Once the country became independent, these persons were quickly discharged because of the traditional dislike by the dominant groups of the north of persons from the southern tribes. In East Africa there is a substantial Indian-Pakistani-Goan minority, which operates almost all retailing and many other types of business and provides most of the personnel for middle-level government jobs (postal clerks, customs and railway operating personnel, and so on). Although many of these families have been in East Africa for several generations, they are not regarded as "Africans"; strong prejudices against them exist, and there is great fear on their part that they will ultimately be uprooted from government jobs and business activity. There have, for example, been anti-Indian boycotts in Uganda, which seriously disrupted trade. In West Africa many of the merchants are Lebanese, and these likewise are the victims of substantial prejudice.

So far as Europeans are concerned, the situation is more complex. In West Africa and Uganda there were virtually no European settlers, and the number in Tanganyika was relatively small. There were, of course, British civil servants and officials of foreign-owned businesses, and the governments have sought to replace the Europeans by Africans as the latter become available; but there is little prejudice, as such, against whites. There are, however, substantial numbers of Europeans in Kenya and Southern Rhodesia, and to a lesser extent in Tanganyika and Northern Rhodesia. There are about 80,000 Europeans in Kenya in farming, government, and business positions; European agriculture has been producing about 80% of the total cash farm income of the country. There are 225,000 Europeans in Southern Rhodesia and 77,000 in Northern Rhodesia. The result has been inevitable racial antagonisms, and currently great fear on the part of the Europeans about their ultimate fate as the Africans gain control of the government; this problem will be discussed in a subsequent section.

Cultural Considerations

Although, as noted, the general cultural background would appear to be more favorable to economic growth than that in many parts of the world, there are several factors in the African scene which are deterrents.

1. The landownership problem. Most land in these countries (outside the European areas) is owned by the tribe or community. The rights of particular families to occupy certain parcels of land and to transmit them to their children are traditionally recognized as a rule, but there is very little private ownership in the usual sense and no possibility of sale of land. This is true even in the larger cities of West Africa, which, outside of Lagos, lack cadastral surveys and title registry.

There are, without question, certain advantages of this system. Profits from land speculation are avoided, as is the landlord problem, so obstructive to economic growth in many countries. The system is favorable to large-scale communal plantation developments on the Israeli model, if a country wishes to encourage this approach. But there are also serious disadvantages from the standpoint of development. Persons have little incentive to make permanent long-range improvements to land that they cannot sell. It is very difficult to obtain land for factory sites; intervention of the national government is often necessary to provide the sites. Property taxes cannot be applied to land, the urban West African cities taxing only improved properties, to the detriment of building. At the same time there is no tradition of the payment of rent by the occupier to the community, except in a few urban areas.

2. Tradition in agricultural methods. Agricultural production remains very primitive, with emphasis on traditional techniques, some of them very wasteful of resources. Change in methods requires a break with long-standing traditions. Change is coming, but it is of necessity slow.

3. Attitudes toward women, and division of functions between men and women. In many areas in these countries, much of the heavy agricultural labor is performed by the women. This frees

the time of the men for other pursuits, such as employment in nearby towns, but it has also resulted in a tradition that the men spend relatively little time at work, a tradition not in the best interests of greater output.

In Ghana and southern Nigeria, women carry on most of the market retail selling (except for the larger stores, which are operated by non-Africans). But in other areas, particularly Moslem areas, such activity—in fact, any economic activity on the part of women outside the household—is contrary to tradition. Particularly in the higher social levels, the wives are not even permitted to appear in public, let alone to carry on economic activity outside the household. It is not meant to argue that Western standards for the role of women are necessarily "better" than the Moslem standards, but the latter are certainly less conducive to economic growth. The generally low esteem in which women are held in many areas also results in the neglect of education for girls.

In sharp contrast, some of the societies, particularly in Nyasaland, are matrilineal, all property passing via the female side. This situation is regarded as an obstacle to improvements in agriculture, since the male members of the family, the best educated, have little interest in improving land over whose future they have no control.

4. The extended family system. One of the most significant characteristics of African society is the extended family—the acceptance of responsibility not only for parents and children, but for brothers and sisters, aunts and uncles, and other less closely related members of the family. A person who succeeds financially may find himself housing and supporting large numbers of less energetic relatives. In a primitive society this form of social insurance is not without advantage. But in the modern economy it may prove a serious deterrent to individual initiative. The practice is held responsible in some areas for the reluctance of persons to put their savings in banks or in business expansion for fear that their relatives will learn of it, and for generally deterring incentives to get ahead.

5. Others. In particular areas there are other practices of obvious disadvantage in terms of economic growth. The pastoral tribes, the Fulani of Nigeria and the Masai of East Africa particularly, regard possession of cattle as the primary evidence of wealth and prestige; the growth of the herd, rather than the sale of the produce, is the primary goal. The result is serious overgrazing and failure to use the products of the cattle to improve the over-all levels of living in the economy. Again, care is needed in making value judgments on such issues, but certainly the practice is a hindrance to economic growth.

PROBLEMS OF EDUCATION
AND TRAINED PERSONNEL

A prime characteristic of underdeveloped economies and a major deterrent to development is the lack of adequate educational facilities, and thus of trained personnel. Low standards of education constitute a major obstacle in the path of the functioning of democracy, and thus indirectly, as well as directly, impede economic growth. It is difficult to summarize the complex and varied picture of educational facilities. Sierra Leone, with perhaps 80% illiteracy and a relatively small percentage of the children of school age attending school, is in the worst position. Ghana, with a compulsory education law and 80% of the children of primary school age (six grades) in school, is in the best position. The similar figure for Uganda is about 60%—but with a wide variation among districts; in remote and primitive Karamoja, scarcely 10% of the children of primary school age are in school.[5] In Tanganyika, only about half of the eligible children enter first grade, most staying in school for four years. The Zanzibar figure is about 30%. The percentages of children obtaining primary education in Eastern and Western Nigeria are nearly as high as in Ghana, even though education is not compulsory. Thus, in Ghana, Nigeria, the mainland East Africa countries, and Rhodesia, from 50 to 80% of the children receive several years of primary education.

The secondary school situation, however, is very much less satisfactory. In Ghana, which has on the whole the most complete educational system, with about 277,000 children entering primary school in 1961, only about 2,500 are completing secondary (high) school, and about 700 the sixth form, which involves two additional years beyond secondary school and prepares for university work. In Uganda, with 60% of the children of primary age in school, less than 1% of those of secondary school age are so enrolled; only 639 children obtained the Cambridge School Certificate, the evidence of successful completion of high school, in 1960.

Finally, at the university level, the number attending is extremely low; in none of the countries would there be more than a few hundred graduates a year, and in most even fewer than this.

One major consequence of the very limited number of trained Africans has been the extensive use of expatriate personnel (and European settlers in Kenya and Rhodesia) for all types of higher-level government and business positions, and in East Africa of Indians for the secondary positions. This, in turn, particularly in East Africa, lessened the pressure in earlier decades to extend

[5] International Bank for Reconstruction and Development, *The Economic Development of Uganda* (Entebbe: Government Printer, 1961), Chapter 12.

African education, since non-Africans were available to fill the jobs. But with the countries independent or becoming independent, there are strong pressures to Africanize government and business jobs. It is almost universally recognized that this cannot be accomplished overnight, and the countries have encouraged expatriate personnel to stay. But these persons see no permanent future in Africa, and thus are anxious, typically, to shift to other positions with better outlook, and the very liberal loss-of-career compensation provided by the British government has encouraged some to leave earlier than they might have otherwise. The settler Europeans and the Indians likewise typically see no future in government, and recruitment of additional persons has become increasingly difficult. Fears of future political instability have made it difficult for Rhodesia to obtain additional employees from European countries or South Africa. The net result is a major problem of transition and the creation of a personnel vacuum which may last for several decades, with consequent deterioration of government services.

All of the governments involved have placed very high priority on increases in educational facilities. The principal gap is the lack of teachers, plus specialized imported equipment for the more advanced schools. Priority has been given to primary education, in an effort to increase literacy and to meet the strongest political pressures. But the flow of teachers through teacher-training channels has been grossly inadequate to staff the new schools—and only by increasing the facilities at the secondary levels can the flow be increased. Thus various expedients have been necessary, including the use of children just out of primary school to teach the beginning grades and of housewives with little education themselves. Secondary schools have relied heavily on expatriate teachers; for example, in Uganda in 1959 of 246 rural secondary school teachers, all except 28 were expatriates. Despite contributions of the Peace Corps and other programs, it is very difficult to build up these staffs adequately. The small number of persons in secondary schools and the relatively large number of university scholarships available have resulted in some countries, such as Ghana and Tanganyika, in virtually all secondary school graduates going on to a university, leaving none available for a wide range of jobs for which this training is needed and adequate.

Another type of problem has been that of effective utilization of the fairly substantial numbers of children who have completed six or eight years of school work but do not go on. This situation has been particularly marked in portions of Nigeria. These boys and girls typically seek to escape from the primitive agriculture of their families, yet their training is insufficient to make them useful in most other occupations. Dissatisfied with return to primitive farm homes, they suffer from a decline in morale and general dissatisfaction. The long-range solution is, of course, the provision of a greater supply of secondary school facilities, so that these children will remain in school for a longer period and will gain sufficient education to be able to fill the numerous positions now inadequately staffed.

PROBLEMS OF COORDINATING ECONOMIC DEVELOPMENT

In common with other economies in relatively early stages of development, the African countries regard as a primary goal the attainment of a rapid rate of growth—one more rapid than would occur if no deliberate efforts to plan development were undertaken. But such forced growth creates a number of problems that would not arise or would take care of themselves under nonforced growth. The major of these can be noted briefly.

The Question of Agriculture

All of these countries are dependent primarily upon agriculture, partly for subsistence and partly for market. But outside of the European farm areas of Kenya and Rhodesia and a few plantations in other countries, most agriculture is extremely primitive, conducted on small plots cultivated by hoe and with little knowledge of modern methods. Mechanization of agriculture, use of fertilizers, development of improved varieties and breeds of cattle, expanded extension programs, and larger-scale operation would bring great potential increases in output with the use of far less man (or woman) power. But a major problem is encountered, that of markets; the basic export products of these areas (cocoa, coffee, cotton, cloves, and other items) are frequently in excessive supply in world markets now, and considerable difficulty would be encountered in selling additional output at profitable prices. Domestic markets for basic farm products have limited potentials. Thus with restricted opportunities to sell greater quantities, mechanization would result largely in the production of current amounts of output in more efficient fashion. What then would become of all the labor that would be freed? If industry and service enterprises were not developed concurrently, the effect would be mass unemployment, growth of urban slums, and general discontent. Thus, while modernization of agriculture is of great importance from a long-range standpoint of economic development, it must not be pushed too fast, and it must be accompanied by simultaneous development of other types of employment. Improvements in agriculture must also of necessity involve larger and consolidated plots, a transition which creates various social and other problems.

Industrial Development

Economic progress must involve development of industry. Unfortunately, many of the countries have only limited resources suitable for manufacturing and thus few types of manufacturing that offer obviously profitable operation. If manufacturing is to be developed to bring greater national output, some form of government selection and assistance appears to be imperative. But particularly in the light of shortages of personnel, such a program is inevitably fraught with dangers centering around the establishment of suitable criteria for selection of industries to be developed. Yet the alternatives are mass unemployment as persons are freed from subsistence agriculture by improved methods, underemployment of various forms, and reliance for payment for imported goods on the export of farm products (whose prices are frequently low relative to cost because of world surpluses and are subject to fluctuation). Few countries in the world today are willing to remain basic material suppliers, but a shift from this situation under the conditions of most African countries requires the most careful planning on the part of governments. One of the dangers is the tendency to stress "prestige" industries such as iron and steel production, even though these are completely uneconomic for the particular country. Another dilemma is that the most profitable industries are frequently those producing cigarettes, liquor, and soft drinks—items not generally given high priority in a development program. It is frequently argued, however, that such industries provide important secondary contributions in building up the supply of skilled labor and management personnel and are therefore justified.

The Degree of Capital Intensity

One of the great potential dangers which faces any country seeking to force rapid economic growth is that of excessive intensification of capital use. High productivity in developed economies is clearly a result of highly capital-intensive techniques—automation and related methods. But in countries with very large labor supplies relative to the amount of capital equipment, the optimum capital-labor relationships are obviously different from the optimum relationships in developed economies. The use of highly capital-intensive methods will aggravate the problem of unemployment and underemployment; while these methods may allow rapid increases in output, only a very small sector of the economy may be benefited,

17

and markets for the goods will be greatly restricted. It is clearly impossible for a country to build a very large stock of capital goods overnight, and in the decades of transition, shifting to excessively capital-intensive methods is certain to produce trouble.

Government versus Private Enterprise

Another basic issue that the countries must resolve is the extent to which government should participate in the actual undertaking of production. In all of these countries, in varying degrees, there is acceptance of the principle that some government participation is required. The slow rate of growth in the past is taken as irrefutable evidence that the government must act to speed up the process, to increase the rate of industrialization, and to direct it to the types of production most significant in terms of economic development. Private investment in production can come only from outside capital or domestic savings. Given the fears of future political instability, the restrictions placed by some countries on foreign firms, and the dislike of foreign domination of the economy, there is a limit to the amount of foreign capital which can be obtained or which the countries are willing to have. But domestic savings are not easily channeled into expansion of production capacity, given the primitive state of the capital markets and the nature of banking in these countries. For example, there is evidence in some countries of excessive use of capital for office building construction. Governments have more effective access to capital markets and to foreign capital sources without danger of foreign domination of the enterprises, and they can bring about the creation of money capital to offset the savings that may be hoarded.

Apart from capital, there is widely accepted in Africa the doctrine that Africans are reluctant to undertake the responsibilities of entrepreneurship, particularly in industrial fields. There is little scientific evidence for this point of view, but the acceptance of it influences government policy in the direction of greater governmental participation in industry. There are, of course, obvious dangers to government participation, which are well known and need not be repeated here.

In practice, the governments have varied in the extent to which they have undertaken industrial development. Ghana is currently going much further than the others, in part because of the acceptance of the philosophy of socialism by the government. There is no present intent in Ghana, however, to nationalize all economic activity. Ghanaian socialism stresses the avoidance of highly unequal income and wealth distribution, the need for provision of education for all and thus more equal opportunity, and government participation in major lines of industry, but encouragement of private enterprise in other fields.

Industry versus Infrastructure

One of the major problems in these countries is that of establishing priorities, since so many things are urgently required. But priorities there must be, and one of the key issues is that of choice between industrial production facilities and so-called infrastructure—roads, railroads, government buildings, and the like. There has been a tendency to concentrate on the latter, partly because projects are more easily selected in this field, partly, perhaps, because of the desire to avoid any danger of competition with private business. The visitor to Africa is impressed with the high quality of many government buildings, university structures, and other features, relative to the primitive nature of much of the country. Without question some of these facilities, such as better roads, are urgently needed for economic development; Latin-American countries, with much higher levels of national income and economic development generally, have frequently suffered from inadequate government development of basic road and utility services. But it appears that the African governments have gone far in the opposite direction.

Foreign Trade

Any rapidly developing economy faces potential foreign exchange problems, although as yet in Africa only Ghana, of the countries being considered, has encountered them. Exports from these countries consist almost entirely of agricultural products, subject to all the vagaries of the world markets for such products, and in many instances to world surplus conditions. Rhodesia, with its copper, is the major exception. Rapid economic growth requires the importation of a great deal of capital equipment, and rising incomes lead to sharp increases in imports of luxury consumption goods which the country cannot produce. The result is the danger of a foreign exchange deficit, particularly if little foreign capital investment is occurring. Ghana, faced with a serious problem of this sort, introduced in 1961 a drastic austerity program, recommended by the English economist Nicholas Kaldor, which included a very high-rate purchase tax (up to $66\frac{2}{3}\%$) on various consumer durables, a compulsory savings program, higher customs duties, and other elements. These encountered strong popular opposition. When exchange difficulties continued, a system of specific import licensing was established, which likewise gave rise to serious operational problems. Substantial question can be raised about the feasibility of such an austerity program, and even its desirability, in terms of effects on incentives. But the primary alternative, that of allowing

19

the foreign exchange value of the money to fall, creates dangers of inflation and lessens confidence of foreign investors.[6]

Ambitions versus Realities

The zeal for economic growth, and the recognition of the need for at least a certain degree of central planning, can easily lead a developing economy into programs which cannot be carried out effectively because of lack of trained personnel. Ghana provides excellent examples of this. In particular, when specific import licensing was introduced in 1961, very serious delays were encountered because of the lack of personnel to handle the applications.

This problem is in a sense an aspect of a basic issue confronting all of these countries as they gain independence. Many elements of British government have been introduced in the years of colonial rule—for example, relatively sophisticated income taxation. These elements have been operated almost solely by expatriate personnel and in some instances, such as the income tax, have affected primarily the non-African population. But as expatriates are replaced by less experienced Africans, and as the complexities of the task increase—for example, as the number of Africans subject to tax grows—the problems of operation may prove almost insurmountable, at least for a number of years.

Special Problems of the Dual Economies

All of the African countries have of course some elements of Western culture and economic systems implanted into them. In West Africa, and to a lesser extent in Uganda, Tanganyika, Zanzibar, and Nyasaland, this element has largely been merged into the African economy. There is no major non-African element of permanent settlers, with an economy essentially of their own, existing alongside the African society. But Rhodesia and Kenya are fundamentally dualistic societies, with a substantial number of Europeans living permanently in the countries, some for several generations, and with modern European cities; Nairobi and Salisbury are among the most modern and attractive cities in the world. The Europeans have developed an agricultural and industrial economy operated on European standards, using, of course, some African labor. Alongside this system is the primitive African society, for the most part far more primitive than that of West Africa, having limited contact with the European economy and still influenced relatively little by it. A high percentage of the national income is produced by a very small percentage of the population. In Rhodesia, the per capita income of Europeans in 1959 was £580 per person,

[6] All the countries under consideration have thus far kept their currencies at par with the British pound sterling.

or $1,624 (the United States figure was $2,166); of Africans about £15 ($42) plus an estimated £11 subsistence income.

The Europeans who had built these modern economies considered themselves to be the appropriate ones to govern as the countries gained their independence. Various color bars grew up over the years, and in Rhodesia a substantial amount of highly restrictive legislation impeded the rise of the African. Southern Rhodesia became a self-governing colony in 1923, and largely dominated the policies of the Federation when it was formed in 1953.

In Kenya the consequence of white domination was the Mau Mau uprisings of the early fifties, and ultimately the granting by Great Britain of a constitution providing for African control of the government. This event, which occurred in 1960, was a great shock to the white minority, which had expected to control the country, and the source of bitter complaints against Great Britian. As a consequence, economic development of Kenya has largely ceased. Residential building construction in Nairobi, for example, fell from an index of 92 in the first quarter of 1960 to 9 in the similar period in 1961. Improvements in farming ceased; and farmers have tended to "mine" their farms to get as much out as quickly as possible and to make plans for leaving. Farms and homes have dropped very sharply in value and are often difficult to sell at any price. The Europeans fear several things: general decline in the quality of schools and other public services; breakdown in law enforcement; actual physical violence; and possible dispossession from their land. Despite some reassurances, statements of African political leaders have been discouraging. Few events in world history have illustrated so dramatically the influence of expectations on investment decisions, since in fact the basic picture, as of 1963, has not yet changed. If confidence is not restored and most Europeans leave, the present economy of Kenya—the industry, the sources of employment, the market for many goods, the tax base, and the exports—will likely collapse, and generations may be required for rebuilding. The basic difficulty lies in the strong conviction on the part of many Europeans that conditions under an African government will be intolerable.

The Rhodesian situation is somewhat different. Nyasaland, with few Europeans and an African government, became determined to withdraw from the Federation and go it alone. But it is a very poor country, one which will have great difficulty in financing current services and development programs. When Northern Rhodesia, which contains the primary copper deposits, gained an African government, it likewise sought its independence. Thus, complete breakup of the Federation became inevitable. Yet from the standpoint of economic development, the common-market element and

other features had great merit. In Southern Rhodesia, there is substantial fear of the future—not yet the panic of Kenya, but strong
doubts about the ability of the Europeans to maintain control of
the government indefinitely—and confidence in the economy has
been seriously weakened. On the other hand, the African political
leaders aggravate the situation by a policy of noncooperation with
the government, although this may in fact be the only effective
means they have to further their political interests.

Workable solutions to the problems of these dual economies—
problems which the United States would have faced had there
been more American Indians—which ensure equity and facilitate
economic development are difficult to devise. The basic principle
of democracy is majority rule, but it is a rule difficult for a minority
to accept when the latter has brought most of the economic development and the majority is made up primarily of uneducated persons
in the lowest income groups—the subsistence farmers and the
lowest-wage workers. Acceptance is particularly difficult when the
African majority has long-standing and often well-justified griev-
ances against the Europeans—in regard to landownership in Kenya
and various forms of restrictive legislation in Rhodesia, for example,
and the color bar generally. The problem is similar to that of South
Africa; the solutions thus far have been very different.[7]

THE FUTURE

The visitor to Africa in 1963 comes away with a generally op-
timistic feeling about the future, the tremendous possibilities for
growth, and the creation of stable democratic societies, with incomes ultimately rising toward the levels of Western Europe, but
also with an awareness of the great problems confronting the countries in attaining this future. The extremely primitive conditions
under which high percentages of the population live, the wretched
slums around some of the West African cities, the primitive methods of agriculture, the limited transport systems, the small sizes of
the markets, the limited resources in some areas, the infancy of
most industry, the complete loss of confidence in the future by the
non-African population in Kenya and the fears in Rhodesia, and
the racial prejudices and discriminations all stress the magnitude
of the tasks of development. Yet the emphasis of the governments

[7] Southern Rhodesia has made progress in recent years in lowering the color
bar, and in increasing opportunities for Africans. It had turned away—slowly,
but nevertheless away—from apartheid as the latter has become increasingly
rigid in South Africa. Unfortunately, the 1962 elections shifted power to a more
conservative group that was less interested in furthering integration.

on education, the great desire of the people for education of their children, the moderation and capability of many of the African leaders, their desire to get high-quality technical assistance from the outside, the well-established British traditions in many aspects of government, and the attempts to ensure democratic government and to protect human rights are all hopeful signs.

A major key to economic growth is political stability—the ability to maintain law and order and the preservation of the rules of democracy and particularly the rights of the minority. This is imperative for the confidence necessary for the expansion of business enterprise. In an electorate in which many voters are still illiterate, in which old wrongs pave the way for demagogues, in which demands for progress are so great that no government can meet all of them, and in which standards of integrity are not as firmly established as they might be, the maintenance of stable governments which function in the interests of the societies as a whole and economic development, rather than the personal interests of the dominant group, is not easily attained.

But without political stability in the sense as used above, economic development cannot be maintained, and in some countries, particularly Kenya, there is danger of retrogression. From the standpoint of trained personnel, some of the countries, particularly in East Africa, would have been better off to postpone independence for five or ten years while much larger numbers of Africans were being trained for responsible positions. But such a policy was not politically possible, and the governments must seek to make the best of the personnel which they can obtain, local and expatriate. The next two decades are the crucial ones for these countries, with great potentials on the one hand and grave dangers on the other.

SELECTED REFERENCES

West Africa

SIERRA LEONE: *Sierra Leone: The Making of a Nation.* Central Office of Information Reference Pamphlet #45. London: H.M.S.O., 1961.

GHANA: Central Bureau of Statistics, *Economic Survey*, annual. Accra: Government Printing Department.

NIGERIA: Royal Institute of International Affairs, *Nigeria: The Political and Economic Background.* Oxford: Oxford University Press, 1960.

International Bank for Reconstruction and Development, *The Economic Development of Nigeria.* Baltimore: The Johns Hopkins University Press, 1955.

Coleman, J. C., *Nigeria: Background to Nationalism.* Berkeley: University of California Press, 1958.

East Africa

Ingham, K., *A History of East Africa*. London: Longmans, 1962.

East Africa: Report of the Economic and Fiscal Commission. London: H.M.S.O., 1961.

International Bank for Reconstruction and Development (volumes published in Baltimore by Johns Hopkins University Press): *The Economic Development of Tanganyika*, 1960, *The Economic Development of Uganda*, 1961, *The Economic Development of Kenya*, 1963.

KENYA: Kenya Ministry of Finance and Development, *Economic Survey*, annual.

Ward, Susan, *Kenya: The Tensions of Progress*, 2nd ed. Oxford: Oxford University Press, 1962.

ZANZIBAR: Selwyn, P., and T. Y. Watson, *Report on the Economic Development of the Zanzibar Protectorate*. Zanzibar: Government Printer, 1962.

TANGANYIKA: *Budget Survey*, annual.

Rhodesia and Nyasaland

Barber, W. J., *The Economy of British Central Africa*. Oxford: Oxford University Press, 1962.

Report of the Advisory Commission on the Review of the Constitution of Rhodesia and Nyasaland. London: H.M.S.O., 1960.

Report on an Economic Survey of Nyasaland. Zomba: Government Printer, 1960.

Ministry of Economic Affairs, Federation of Rhodesia and Nyasaland, *Economic Report*, annual.

General

Hicks, U. K., *Development from Below*. Oxford: Oxford University Press, 1961.

Hicks, U. K., *et al.*, *Federalism and Economic Growth in Underdeveloped Countries*. London: George Allen & Unwin, Ltd., 1961.

Kimble, G. H. T., *Tropical Africa*, 2 vols. New York: Twentieth Century Fund, 1960.

2 The Tax Structures[1]

WITH A COMMON BACKGROUND of British colonial rule, over periods ranging from sixty years to a century and a half, the tax systems of the eight African countries in this study have a substantial common-denominator element; however, it has been growing less important as the countries have been adjusting their tax systems according to their particular circumstances. This chapter will present a brief summary of the tax structures.

TAX COLLECTIONS AS A PERCENTAGE OF GROSS PRODUCT

Table 2.1 shows annual tax collection expressed as a percentage of gross domestic product at factor prices. While the product figures are only estimates, the percentages are of some significance. A relatively high degree of uniformity is noted, the range being only from 9% to 14%, outside of Zanzibar (17%). It will be noted that the four countries with the highest percentages are the four which have the highest gross product per capita figures. The relative importance of taxation is much lower than in more highly developed countries, where the comparable figures range between 20 and 35%.

[1] Portions of the material in this chapter appeared in the September–October, 1962, issue of the *Canadian Tax Journal*, in the article entitled "Taxation in Tropical Africa," and are reproduced by permission of the Canadian Tax Foundation.

TABLE 2.1   TOTAL TAX COLLECTIONS EXPRESSED AS A PERCENTAGE
OF GROSS DOMESTIC PRODUCT AT FACTOR PRICES, 1960–
1961

Country	Percentage
Zanzibar	17
Rhodesia	14
Ghana	13*
Kenya	12
Uganda	11
Nigeria	9
Tanganyika	9

* Expressed as percentage of GDP at market prices.
Taxes include territorial as well as federal tax collections in the federal countries.
Local taxes, which constitute a relatively small percentage of the total taxes, are
excluded because data are incomplete.

RELATIVE RELIANCE ON DIRECT
AND INDIRECT TAXES

Table 2.2 indicates the relative reliance of the countries (including both federal and territorial governments in the federal
states) on direct and indirect taxes. One problem in classification
arises. Export taxes, which are significant in five of the countries,

TABLE 2.2   RELATIVE RELIANCE ON DIRECT, INDIRECT, AND EXPORT
TAXES, 1961–1962

Country	Percentage of Tax Revenue from		
	Direct Taxes	Indirect Taxes	Export Duties
Rhodesia	67	33	0
Kenya	44	56	0
Tanganyika	30	70	negl.
Sierra Leone	30	63	7
Uganda	24	61	15
Nigeria	21	65	14
Ghana	15	66	19
Zanzibar	10	45	45

take the technical form of indirect taxes, but are widely regarded
as constituting levies on the incomes of the producers of the products.
Accordingly, these are listed as a third and distinct form.

The Rhodesian figure of 67% of revenue from direct taxes is
one of the highest in the world, being comparable to those in the
United States, Sweden, and the Netherlands, and much higher

than in the United Kingdom or Canada. On the other hand, for six of the eight countries the figure is 30% or less, and thus much lower than in the more highly developed areas. The two countries with heavy reliance on income taxation are those with the largest European populations. While even in these countries the Europeans comprise only a small percentage of the population, they bear most of the burden of the income taxes. If the export taxes are regarded as direct taxes, Zanzibar would also have over half of its revenue from this type of tax, and the West African countries and Uganda would show greater relative reliance on it.

THE DIRECT TAXES

The breakdown of the yield from direct taxes is shown in Table 2.3. The special forms are primarily levies on the royalties of mining and petroleum operations.

TABLE 2.3 PERCENTAGE OF TOTAL DIRECT TAX REVENUE GAINED FROM VARIOUS FORMS OF DIRECT TAXES, 1961–1962

Country	Company Taxes	Special Forms	Personal Income Tax	Personal (Poll) Tax
Ghana	76	16	8	0
Sierra Leone	63	28	9	0
Rhodesia	61	0	31	8
Nigeria	24	40	36	0
Tanganyika	43	0	37	20
Uganda	42	0	42	16
Kenya	38	0	48	14
Zanzibar	10	0	90	0

Thus the company and special taxes—which are also largely on companies—are of primary importance in Sierra Leone, Rhodesia, Ghana, and Nigeria. In Tanganyika and Uganda the yields of the personal and company income taxes are about the same, and in Kenya the personal tax is more important. In all three of these countries the combined personal income and personal (poll) taxes exceed the company tax in yield. In Zanzibar the company tax provides only 10% of the total.

All eight countries impose both personal and company taxes; the four East African countries have a common income tax structure (with minor exceptions) and joint administration. Distinct from the income taxes are the personal taxes, which have developed from the flat-rate hut taxes initially imposed primarily to induce persons to enter the commercial sector of the economy by sale of produce or by seeking employment. They are used in all the juris-dictions noted except Zanzibar, either by the central or local governments or both. They are integrated with the income taxes in Eastern and Western Nigeria but elsewhere are operated distinctly from them, and persons are subject to both levies if their incomes are high enough (except in Northern Nigeria).

THE INDIRECT TAXES

Table 2.4 shows the relative importance of the three major types of indirect taxes: customs duties, excises, and others—mainly motor vehicle and other licenses.

TABLE 2.4   MAJOR INDIRECT TAXES, 1961

| | Percentage of Total Indirect Tax Revenue from | | |
Country	Customs	Excises	Licenses and Miscellaneous
Zanzibar	98	0	2
Sierra Leone	96	negl.	4
Nigeria	89	10	1
Ghana	84	9	7
Tanganyika	70	21	9
Rhodesia	69	18	13
Uganda	64	28	8
Kenya	61	22	17

Customs duties are the largest single source of revenue in all of the countries except Rhodesia; they yield over half the revenue in Sierra Leone, Ghana, and Nigeria, and together, with excises, in Uganda and Tanganyika. Relative to customs, the excises are of much greater importance in the mainland East African countries and Rhodesia than they are elsewhere, mainly because domestic production of goods subject to excises is more significant in these countries. Only in Kenya and Rhodesia are licenses and other miscellaneous items of major significance.

Customs

The heavy reliance on customs duties follows the worldwide pattern on this question; in countries in which a high percentage of goods other than basic staples is imported, and the levels of do-mestic commercial activities and of education are relatively low, the customs duty is the simplest means of collecting most govern-ment revenue. The pattern in Table 2.4 shows likewise the tendency for countries to move away from customs, partly to excises, but in large measure to direct taxes, as their economies develop.

Excises

The excise systems are limited to a relatively few commodities traditionally subject: cigarettes, beer, liquor, and motor fuel. There are no general sales taxes in these countries, and no extended excise system covering luxury goods; the Ghana purchase tax is (except for motor vehicles) a supplement to the customs duty. No close tie has been developed between the yield of excises or customs duties on motor fuel and highway expenditure, but the high taxes on these items are justified on the grounds of their contribution to road building.

Export Duties

Several of the countries in this group have long been major users of export duties, applying to exports of staple commodities. Zanzibar obtains nearly half of its revenue from the export duty on cloves; and export taxes are important in Ghana, Nigeria, and Uganda. Administration of these taxes is very simple because the products are exported through marketing boards.

LOCAL TAXATION

Local government finance has developed rather slowly in Africa, although great progress has been made in recent years. In the larger cities, property taxes are employed. In Ghana the tax applies only to buildings, on a replacement cost basis; in Nigeria improved properties are taxed on an annual rental value basis in the British tradition. In Uganda and Rhodesia a differential rate system sharply favoring buildings over land is employed, and in Kenya and Tanganyika only the site value is taxed. There are no rural land taxes except low-rate levies in parts of Uganda. The other major local tax is the personal tax, noted above. Local license taxes are levied, and in some countries taxes known as cesses are imposed on the local sale of produce in the markets.

FINANCIAL ASPECTS OF FEDERALISM

It is difficult to summarize the financial arrangements of the Nigerian and Rhodesian federations in any simple way, but a few key points will be noted. In Nigeria, the Federal government has exclusive jurisdiction over customs, excise, and export duties; sales and purchase taxes with a few exceptions; taxation of companies; mining royalties; and incomes of the residents of the Federal District of Lagos. The regional governments have the power to tax personal incomes, subject to the general requirements of the Income Tax Management Act imposed by the Federal government; poll or personal taxes; license taxes; and taxes on property. The Federal government collects about 85% of all tax revenues of the country, but distributes about half to the regions, which in turn thus get about 80% of their total revenue from the Federal government.

In Rhodesia, even greater centralization of revenue collection is attained. The Federation has exclusive jurisdiction over customs and excises (except on motor fuels) and both personal and corporate income taxes. The territories can and do (with the exception of Northern Rhodesia on personal income tax) levy 20% federally collected surcharges on the Federation income taxes. The only major tax revenues collected by the territories are the personal (poll) taxes, and various licenses. Thus the Federation collects 76% of the territorial revenues and 89% of the combined federal-territorial revenue.

In East Africa, the customs duties and income taxes are jointly administered through the Common Services Organization, and the revenue is returned to the countries on the basis of origin (i.e., in the instance of customs, destination of the goods). About 83% of the revenues of the countries are jointly administered, the personal taxes, export duties (significant only in Uganda), and license taxes being the only major taxes administered by the countries themselves.

3   Income Taxation: Structure[1]

THE EXPERIENCE of the eight countries with income taxation is of interest not only in terms of the countries themselves but for the light that the experience may throw on the use of income taxation in developing economies generally. This is a question that has received major attention in other parts of the world—for example, Latin America—in recent years. There are several major questions that arise with regard to the use of income taxation in such economies. One question is that of administrative feasibility, given the limited numbers of trained administrators and the relatively inadequate general level of record keeping and education. Others relate to the most satisfactory structure of income taxation under such conditions, the most appropriate types of enforcement programs, and the broader economic questions of the relative effects of income and other taxation on economic development, which will be considered in Chapter 9.

Sierra Leone and Ghana had for a time a single uniform income tax with joint administration. However, administration was ultimately separated, and the taxes have gradually diverged substantially; that of Sierra Leone bears the greatest resemblance to the original. In Nigeria, which has a federal governmental structure,

[1] Portions of Chapters 3 and 4 appeared in the July–August, September–October, and November–December, 1963, issues of the *British Tax Review*, and are reproduced by permission.

the field of income taxation is now divided among the four governments. There is a single company tax, imposed and administered by the Federal government, covering the entire country. Taxation of individual incomes, however, rests by terms of the constitution with the regional governments, although the Federal government has the power to lay down general rules relating to structure (but not rates or allowances). In conformity with this power, the Income Tax Management Act was imposed in 1961. The four individual taxes, a federally imposed tax for the Federal territory of Lagos, and those levied by the governments of Western, Northern, and Eastern Nigeria, vary substantially in rates and other features.

In East Africa the situation is in a sense reversed. A common income tax is employed by Uganda, Tanganyika, Kenya, and Zanzibar. The basic act is imposed by the East Africa Legislative Assembly, the joint legislative body of the first three countries named, with a similar separately levied act in Zanzibar. The rates and allowances are imposed by separate legislation in each of the four countries, but in fact are identical except for minor differences. Administration is under the jurisdiction of the East Africa Common Services Organization (until 1961 the East Africa High Commission). In Rhodesia, both company and personal income taxes are levied and administered by the Federation government, with 20% surcharges (also collected by the Federation) imposed by the three territorial governments, except for the personal income tax in Northern Rhodesia.

The oldest of these taxes is that of Rhodesia, which was first introduced in 1918 in Southern Rhodesia, and carried over with minor changes to the Federation when the latter was formed in 1953. Nigerian income taxation in modern form began in 1940, although there was a simplified type of tax dating back to 1927, and Northern Nigeria was one of the first sections in Africa to use direct personal taxation, under the Fulani Emirs prior to the advent of the British. Kenya introduced the income tax in 1937, after previous attempts in 1921 and 1931 failed in the face of strong opposition. The other three East African countries levied the tax in 1940, and Ghana and Sierra Leone in 1943.

Except for the tax of Southern Rhodesia, which was modeled after the South African tax, all of these income taxes were originally based upon the Colonial Model Income Tax Ordinance, prepared in 1922 by an Interdepartmental Committee in the United Kingdom for use in "colonies not possessing responsible government." Despite subsequent modifications, United Kingdom case law and tax guides are applicable to a substantial extent in these countries, except Rhodesia, where South African case law is applicable.

This chapter will review the structure, rates, allowances, and other features of the taxes. The next chapter will summarize their operation.

TAXABLE INCOME

All these income taxes are global rather than schedular in nature, all income in the usual sense of that term being lumped and treated as a unit at a uniform rate regardless of source. Special rules are provided for certain types of income:

1. Foreign income. A major issue is that of localization of income. Within the three federal or semifederal jurisdictions, the residence rule is basic for personal income tax liability, and double taxation is entirely prevented. Company taxation liability depends upon origin of the earnings, with no double taxation.

So far as foreign income is concerned, the African countries are more liberal than many others. In Sierra Leone, Nigeria, and Ghana, income earned outside the country is taxable only if brought into the country. Double-taxation relief is provided in Sierra Leone and Nigeria for Commonwealth countries and several others with which treaties have been signed. Ghana is negotiating agreements currently with several countries. In East Africa (since 1961) and Rhodesia, such income is not subject to tax.[2] The exemption rule is designed largely for simplification of administration but is sometimes charged with encouraging persons to invest outside their home country.

2. Capital gains. In agreement with past British practice, capital gains are taxable. The exact delineation of such gains from taxable business profit varies somewhat but in general is based upon intent of purchase as the primary criterion. If capital equipment is sold by business firms for a figure in excess of the depreciated value, the gain up to the amount of depreciation that has been allowed is taxable. In East Africa any amount in excess of original cost is taxable.

3. Rental value of owner-occupied housing. Rental values were taxable in East Africa until 1961, when the rule was abandoned as a part of a program to simplify the tax. Thus at present such income is not taxable in any of the countries.

4. Supplements to wages and salaries. The general policy is to tax allowances for quarters, board, servants, rations, power, etc., and in most countries to tax the value of such items provided by the employer to employees. Rhodesia and Ghana, for example, have a

[2] In Rhodesia, interest from outside sources is taxable, and dividends are subject to supertax. Rhodesia has tax treaties with 12 countries.

broad coverage, including the value of quarters, board and lodging, servants, rations, etc. Sierra Leone taxes the value of light, fuel, and servants, but not board and lodging. Nigeria taxes the allowances, but not the value of such services provided by the employer. East Africa for a time included all fringe benefits of any kind provided by the employer, including the value of trips on free passes on the railways, but in 1961, in order to simplify administration, exempted the first £50 of such allowances. In East Africa the value of housing provided is defined to be one tenth of the person's wage or salary, with a maximum of £250.

5. Exempt incomes. The traditional exemptions of income of various governmental, religious, charitable, and similar organizations are provided (but contributions to such organizations are not deductible, except to a restricted extent in Rhodesia). In addition, a few other types of incomes are specifically excluded. Ghana exempts the income of cocoa farmers, whose products are subject to an export levy, and Zanzibar did not tax any farm income until recent years. Interest on government savings certificates and post office savings deposits are typically exempt.

As of 1963, there are no longer any exemptions by racial groups, as was common in the past. Africans were exempt from income tax in Uganda until 1961, and non-Africans were subject to Federal rather than regional tax in Nigeria until 1961.

6. Dividends. Except for Ghana and the East African corporation tax, these countries have followed the earlier British practice with regard to dividends. The company tax is regarded essentially as a means of collecting, at the company level, the tax on the dividends. The individual must include in his income the dividend and the tax paid by the company on the dividend. He then receives a credit against his tax for the tax which has been paid on the dividend element at the company level, and thus double taxation is avoided.

Ghana, under its new simplified income tax, taxes dividends fully, except for those subject to pioneer companies and small companies legislation, for which there is partial exemption. In East Africa, the corporation tax introduced in 1962 is not credited to shareholders.

PRESUMPTIVE INCOME

When the Ghanaian income tax was subjected to basic reforms in 1961, a presumptive income rule was introduced. For traders and similar business activities, the figure of taxable income cannot be less than $2\frac{1}{2}\%$ of gross turnover. If the actual net figure is less, the tax rate is applied to the $2\frac{1}{2}\%$ gross figure. Thus an element of a turnover tax is introduced into the law to ensure some minimum payment by all businesses, a rule which increases the potentially adverse effect of the tax on risk taking. Likewise, professional men are taxed on figures based on typical incomes for the particular occupations unless records demonstrate that the liability should be less.

BUSINESS EXPENSES

The rules relating to business expenses are comparable to those of other countries. The East African law is slightly more restrictive, confining deductible expenses to those incurred in "production of income" rather than for "purposes of business." The difference is not significant in practice.

The major issues arise with respect to depreciation allowances, the rules being typically more liberal than traditional British depreciation practice.

So far as buildings are concerned, all of the countries permit deduction of depreciation charges except Sierra Leone, which confines the deduction to industrial buildings, and Rhodesia, which limits it to industrial and farm buildings. Both Ghana and Nigeria provide the very liberal authorization of 10% a year for all buildings. East Africa confines the figure to 4% a year except for 6% on hotels. On equipment the basic rule is to adjust the figure in terms of actual expected life. East Africa establishes three classes of equipment for depreciation purposes: tractors and similar equipment, $37\frac{1}{2}$%; power-driven vehicles, 25%; all other machinery and plant, $12\frac{1}{2}$%. The figure for farm equipment is 20%. Ghana, Nigeria, and Rhodesia provide liberal allowances for mines: 15% in the first two mentioned, 20% in Rhodesia.

Apart from the basic rules, Ghana, Nigeria, and Rhodesia all provide liberal *initial allowances* for the year in which investments are made. For buildings the figures are 10% in Ghana and Rhodesia (industrial buildings, farm improvements, railway lines, and African housing), 20% in Nigeria on industrial buildings and none on others. For plant equipment the figures are 40% in Ghana and Nigeria, 20% in Rhodesia. For mining companies the figures are 20% in Ghana, 25% in Nigeria. For plantations and farms the figure is 25% in Ghana, 100% in East Africa for clearing of land and making of permanent improvements, 20% in Rhodesia on farm equipment. Uganda allows 100% initial depreciation on buildings for the coffee industry. These initial allowances reduce the allowable depreciation in subsequent years.

Rhodesia and East Africa, however, also provide *investment allowances*, which do not reduce the subsequent deductible amounts. In Rhodesia, the allowance is 10% on manufacturing machinery and equipment. Thus in total, in Rhodesia, the first year's allowance is 38% of the cost of the equipment. In 1962, East Africa replaced its initial allowance by an investment allowance of 10% on manufacturing machinery and plant. All of the countries permit obsolescence deductions when equipment is scrapped before being fully depreciated.

All of the countries permit some transfer of losses. Nigeria and Rhodesia provide the same rule: unrestricted carry-forward but no carry-back. Ghana limits the carry-forward to 15 years; none is allowed on trade. East Africa permits one year's carry-back and unrestricted carry-forward; Sierra Leone permits one year's carry-back, six years' carry-forward. The unrestricted carry-forward rule has great merit in reducing the adverse effect of the tax on business investment.

PERSONAL ALLOWANCES

Despite the common British colonial background of these countries, there are wide variations in the personal allowance systems. At the one extreme, Western and Eastern Nigeria provide no basic personal exemption at all, and thus require payment of a minimum tax from all adult males, with administrative discretion to exempt persons unable to pay. However, the tax is adjusted in terms of numbers of dependents. Sierra Leone, while providing an exemption for the basic income tax, supplements the basic tax with a minimum tax without the usual allowances on all incomes over £200. The Nigeria-Lagos income tax is supplemented by a separate income "rate" with minimum payment by all adults. In most of the other jurisdictions there are universal personal taxes separate from the income tax, as explained in Chapter 5.

Of the countries that provide personal allowances for the taxpayer, in all except Rhodesia, the system takes the form of a deduction from income, and thus the monetary significance of the allowance varies with the income. Rhodesia provides, instead, a credit against tax (called a rebate), which yields a uniform tax saving for persons in all taxable income levels. The allowance systems also vary in one other major regard: in Ghana and Northern Nigeria provision is made for a single consolidated allowance regardless of family status. The figure is £240 in Ghana. It is £240 in Northern Nigeria for those with income in excess of £400; those with income under £400 are not subject to income tax, but to community (personal) tax only. Of the countries with allowances for dependents, Sierra Leone and Nigeria-Lagos provide allowances for the taxpayer of £300, East Africa of £225. The Rhodesia rebate (tax credit) is £25, which is equivalent to a £400 personal allowance for the first rate bracket (ignoring territorial tax supplements).

The treatment of women, single and married, varies and has deviated in substantial degree from standard European practice, in large measure because of long-standing African traditions of not taxing women. Three of the taxes—those of Sierra Leone, East Africa, and Rhodesia—require that husband and wife combine their incomes; all three provide additional allowances for a wife. The combined amount for husband and wife is less than double that for a single person in Sierra Leone and Rhodesia, and more than double in East Africa. Sierra Leone provides an additional £200 for the wife (and a special £500 earned income allowance on her income); Rhodesia provides a tax credit (rebate) of £37 10s. for a married couple instead of the £25 for a single person.[3] East Africa provides a £700 figure instead of the £225, with an intermediate £450 figure for the head of a household who is not married.

In Ghana, and under the four Nigerian governments, husband and wife are not required to combine their incomes and may be treated as separate taxpayers. In Ghana, the husband receives no additional allowance for a wife, but the wife is entitled to a £240 allowance so far as her own income is concerned. Northern Nigeria provides a married woman the same £240 so far as her own income is concerned; Western Nigeria, with no allowance for a single man, provides a £300 allowance for a single woman, and £200 for a married couple, if the wife is not herself a taxpayer. Eastern Nigeria provides a special allowance of £100 so far as women employees' income is concerned; women traders in six urban areas are also taxable; other women are exempt. Eastern Nigeria has built into its tax tables a reduction in tax for married couples as compared to single persons. The value of the reduction is not a uniform amount; it rises as income rises, but not proportionately. Lagos, which gives the same £300 exemption for men as for women, allows an additional £100 for the wife, whether she has her own income or not. The practice of providing higher allowances for women with their own income than for men is an outgrowth of the tradition of taxing only men. But there is a definite tendency to move away from it, as witnessed by its absence in two of the newest income tax acts, those of Nigeria-Lagos and Northern Nigeria.

ALLOWANCES FOR CHILDREN AND OTHER DEPENDENTS

Ghana and Northern Nigeria, with their consolidated allowance systems, provide no additional allowances for children, although the latter does so indirectly by providing for an educational allowance.

[3] However, in terms of income, this figure represents £800, or double that for a single person.

The other countries provide direct allowances. Figures for Sierra Leone are £50 for children in the country, £100 for those outside; in Western Nigeria £40; in Nigeria-Lagos £60. Eastern Nigeria has a varying figure, one which rises with income but less than proportionately. In East Africa the allowance varies with the age of the child as follows: age under six, £75; six to twelve, £100; twelve to nineteen, £150; £250 if over seventeen and at a university. This adjustment is made in lieu of the educational allowance withdrawn in 1961. Rhodesia uses a flat figure of £22 10s. tax credit (rebate), a substantial sum in terms of tax saving for the lower-income groups. Unlike United States practice, an age maximum is set, typically sixteen (twenty-one in Rhodesia), applying unless the child is in school or a university (and in some instances in apprenticeship). All countries except Sierra Leone and Rhodesia limit the number of allowances for children to four—a measure designed to protect the revenue in the case of very large families. Although multiple wives are common in some of the countries (particularly Northern Nigeria), in no instance is an allowance provided for the additional wives. In Rhodesia the income of the children must be included in the taxpayer's income if it is derived from property placed in their names.

Allowances for dependent relatives are provided in Sierra Leone (£100), Northern Nigeria and Nigeria-Lagos (£100), Western Nigeria (actual expenditure up to £50), and in Rhodesia a tax credit (rebate) of £15 if the support is from £50 to £150, and £22 10s. if more than £150. The number of such dependent allowances usually is restricted.

Several other allowances, in large measure copied from British practice, include:

1. Insurance premiums and contributions to pension systems, in Sierra Leone, the four Nigerian jurisdictions, East Africa, and Rhodesia (life insurance and personal accident insurance only), in all instances subject to certain maxima and other restrictions.

2. Educational expenses for dependent children, in Western Nigeria, Northern Nigeria (university or other education outside Nigeria), and Nigeria-Lagos (amounts spent in excess of £60, up to £90), and in Zanzibar, which did not follow the action of the other East African countries in 1961 in eliminating this deduction. The educational allowance was designed during the colonial period primarily for the benefit of British civil servants, rather than for conditions peculiar to present-day Africa.

3. Deductions for passage to Africa, designed largely for British civil servants, still provided in Northern Nigeria, East Africa, and Sierra Leone, with varying rules.

4. Medical and related expenses, 3 shillings per pound paid in excess of £50, up to a maximum of £22 10s., in Rhodesia only. Rhodesia is also the only country to provide special allowances for appliances for physically disabled and allowances for the blind. Kenya and Zanzibar alone provide additional allowances for old people; prior to 1961, Tanganyika and Uganda did so as well. The failure of Kenya to make the change is the source of one of the very few present-day nonuniformities in the East African income tax.

RATES

Table 3.1 presents a relatively detailed statement of the rate structures. Care must be taken, however, in making comparisons, because of differing personal allowance systems. Thus the Western Nigeria and Eastern Nigeria initial rates apply from the first pound of income, so far as adult males are concerned (single males, in Western Nigeria). The Rhodesia rates are likewise applicable from the first pound of income, because the personal allowances take the credit-against-tax form.

Rhodesia uses a double-rate structure, of normal tax and surtax (supertax), the latter applying only to persons whose incomes exceed £2,000 for single persons and £4,000 for married persons. For persons subject, the supertax applies to the entire income, but with a rebate which, in effect, limits the application of the tax to the amounts above the figures indicated. All of the other taxes now use a single-rate structure, with each successive rate applying to the income in excess of the bracket figure. However, Eastern Nigeria has one of the most curious rate structures of any income tax, one which produces 100% marginal rates at various incomes. For all incomes up to £3,000, which includes most taxpayers (all except 45, in 1958), the amount of tax for each successive £10 bracket of income is specified, instead of percentage rates. Four columns are provided; for single taxpayers, for married persons with no children, for those with one or two children, and for those with three or more children. The rates shown in Table 3.1 for Eastern Nigeria are calculated marginal rates for the various figures, and are by no means entirely comparable to those for the other taxing jurisdictions.

In all other instances, the tax rate tables take the usual form, with marginal rates applying to the income in excess of the bracket figures. No two of the structures are exactly alike; but typically the number of brackets is relatively small, from 7 in Sierra Leone to 14 in East Africa. The first brackets are typically £400 or £500 in size, the top brackets larger, with the maximum rate applying to incomes in excess of £4,300 in Western Nigeria, £5,000 in Northern Nigeria, £6,000 in Rhodesia, £9,000 in East Africa, £6,960 in Ghana,

TABLE 3.1   INCOME TAX RATES, 1963,* IN PERCENTAGES

Taxable Income† (pounds)	Sierra Leone	Ghana	Western Nigeria	Northern Nigeria
1 to 100	2½	1¼	3¾	6¼
101 to 200	2½	1¼	3¾	6¼
201 to 300	2½	1¼^b	3¾	6¼
301 to 400	2½	2½	3¾	6¼
401 to 500	5	2½^c	3¾	6¼
501 to 600	5	3¾	4⅙	8¾
601 to 700	5	3¾	4⅙	8¾
701 to 800	5	3¾^d	5	8¾
801 to 900	12½	5	5	8¾
901 to 1000	12½	5	10	8¾
1001 to 1100	12½	5	10	15
1101 to 1200	12½	5	15	15
1201 to 1300	25	7½	15	15
1301 to 1400	25	7½	15	15
1401 to 1500	25	7½	15	15
1501 to 1600	25	7½	15	20
1601 to 1700	25	7½^e	20	20
1701 to 1800	25	10	20	20
1801 to 1900	37½	10	20	20
1901 to 2000	37½	10	20	20
2001 to 2300	37½	10^f	20	25
2301 to 2500	37½	12½	25	25
2501 to 2600	37½	12½	25	25
2601 to 2800	50	12½	25	25
2801 to 3000	50	12½^g	25	25
3001 to 3300	50	15	25	32½
3301 to 3800	50	15	35	32½
3801 to 4000	50	15^h	35	32½
4001 to 4300	50	20	35	40
4301 to 4800	50	20	45	40
4801 to 5000	50	20	45	40
5001 to 6000	50	20^i	45	50
6001 to 7000	50	25^j	45	50
7001 to 8000	50	30	45	50
8001 to 9000	50	30	45	50
9001 to 10000	50	30	45	50
10001 and over	75^a	30	45	50

* As of April 1.
† After deduction of personal and other allowances.
a. 50% to 10,600, thence 75%
b. to 240, thence 2½%
c. to 480, thence 3¾%
d. to 720, thence 5%
e. to 1680, thence 10%
f. to 2160, thence 12½%
g. to 2880, thence 15%
h. to 3840, thence 20%
i. to 5040, thence 25%
j. to 6960, thence 30%

Table 3.1 (Continued)

Taxable Income† (pounds)	Eastern Nigeria[k] (Single Person)	Nigeria-Lagos	East Africa	Rhodesia and Nyasaland Federation Tax[l] Married	Single
1 to 100	4.37	5	10	$3\frac{3}{4}$	$6\frac{1}{4}$
101 to 200	4.37	5	10	$3\frac{3}{4}$	$6\frac{1}{4}$
201 to 300	6.87	5	10	$3\frac{3}{4}$	$6\frac{1}{4}$
301 to 400	6.87	5	10	$3\frac{3}{4}$	$6\frac{1}{4}$
401 to 500	6.87	10	15	$3\frac{3}{4}$	$6\frac{1}{4}$
501 to 600	6.87	10	15	$6\frac{1}{4}$	10
601 to 700	6.87	$12\frac{1}{2}$	15	$6\frac{1}{4}$	10
701 to 800	6.87	$12\frac{1}{2}$	15	$6\frac{1}{4}$	10
801 to 900	13.12	$17\frac{1}{2}$	20	$6\frac{1}{4}$	10
901 to 1000	14.37	$17\frac{1}{2}$	20	$6\frac{1}{4}$	10
1001 to 1100	15.62	$22\frac{1}{2}$	20	10	15
1101 to 1200	16.87	$22\frac{1}{2}$	20	10	15
1201 to 1300	18.12	$22\frac{1}{2}$	25	10	15
1301 to 1400	19.37	$22\frac{1}{2}$	25	10	15
1401 to 1500	20.62	$22\frac{1}{2}$	25	10	15
1501 to 1600	21.87	$22\frac{1}{2}$	25	15	$22\frac{1}{2}$
1601 to 1700	23.12	$22\frac{1}{2}$	30	15	$22\frac{1}{2}$
1701 to 1800	24.37	$22\frac{1}{2}$	30	15	$22\frac{1}{2}$
1801 to 1900	25.62	30	30	15	$22\frac{1}{2}$
1901 to 2000	26.87	30	30	15	$22\frac{1}{2}$
2001 to 2300	28.12	30	35	$22\frac{1}{2}$	34.9
2301 to 2500	31.87	30	35	$22\frac{1}{2}$	34.9
2501 to 2600	31.87	30	40	27	34.9
2601 to 2800	31.87	30	40	27	34.9
2801 to 3000	31.87	$37\frac{1}{2}$	40	27	34.9
3001 to 3300	35.00	$37\frac{1}{2}$	45	27	36.2
3301 to 3800	35.00	$37\frac{1}{2}$	45	27	36.2
3801 to 4000	35.00	$46\frac{1}{4}$	45	27	36.2
4001 to 4300	42.5	$46\frac{1}{4}$	50	38.7	38.7
4301 to 4800	42.5	$46\frac{1}{4}$	50	38.7	38.7
4801 to 5000	42.5	$57\frac{1}{2}$	50	38.7	38.7
5001 to 6000	45.00	$57\frac{1}{2}$	55	42.4	42.4
6001 to 7000	45.00	$57\frac{1}{2}$	60	47.4	47.4
7001 to 8000	45.00	$57\frac{1}{2}$	65	47.4	47.4
8001 to 9000	45.00	$57\frac{1}{2}$	70	47.4	47.4
9001 to 10000	45.00	$57\frac{1}{2}$	75	47.4	47.4
10001 and over	56.25	75	75	47.4	47.4

k. Rates not expressed in Act. Marginal figures calculated from rate tables.
l. Plus 20 per cent surcharge in Nyasaland and Southern Rhodesia.

£10,000 in Eastern Nigeria and Nigeria-Lagos, and £10,600 in Sierra Leone.

By far the highest initial rate is the 10% figure of East Africa, but this tax has a relatively high exemption: £700 for a married couple. The other initial figures range from $1\frac{1}{4}$% in Ghana and $2\frac{1}{2}$% in Sierra Leone to $6\frac{1}{4}$% for a single person in Rhodesia, plus the 20% surcharge in Southern Rhodesia and Nyasaland. The lowest over-all levy is that of Ghana, with a rate which rises very slowly, and the lowest maximum (30%). Nigeria-Lagos and East Africa have the heaviest over-all figures (though not at every income level).

The top rate is 75%, in three jurisdictions: Sierra Leone (income in excess of £10,600), Nigeria-Lagos (£10,000), and East Africa (£9,000). The top figure is approximately 61% in Rhodesia (including the territorial surcharge of Southern Rhodesia and Nyasaland), $56\frac{1}{4}$% in Eastern Nigeria, 50% in Northern Nigeria, 45% in Western Nigeria, and 30% in Ghana. These top brackets are not of great significance; in 1959, for example, there were 91 persons in Kenya subject to the top rate (out of about 50,000 taxpayers), 26 in Tanganyika, 24 in Uganda, 3 in Zanzibar. In 1957–1958 there were 45 taxpayers in Eastern Nigeria in the top bracket (over £3,000). In Rhodesia in 1959, there were 949 taxpayers subject to the top rate, out of a total of 74,328.

THE MINIMUM TAXES

In Sierra Leone and all four areas of Nigeria, a minimum tax is collected, regardless, except in Sierra Leone, of how low the income is. Actually, administrative discretion to exempt the destitute is usually provided. In Sierra Leone, all persons with income of £201 or more are subject to a graduated tax ranging from £3 on incomes between £210 and £300 to £100 on incomes in excess of £2,700; this must be paid in addition to the income tax proper (first schedule), and is levied on total income after business expenses, without personal allowances or other deductions. It is thus designed to ensure some tax payment by all income groups except the very lowest.

In Nigeria the system varies with the regions. In the north, all employees pay a minimum tax of $2\frac{1}{2}$% on their total income without personal allowances, while nonemployees with low incomes pay the community personal tax rather than the income tax. In Western Nigeria it is assumed that all adult males earn at least £50, and thus they pay a minimum tax of £1 7/6; there are no personal allowances for incomes under £300. In Eastern Nigeria there is a minimum tax of £1 7/6 for all adult males. In Nigeria-Lagos, all persons, male or female, with any income pay a minimum income "rate" (distinguished from the income tax) of 10s., and those with incomes in excess of £100 pay on a graduated scale with a maximum of £4 on all income in excess of £203; this is paid in addition to income tax for persons subject to the latter.

In Ghana, East Africa, and Rhodesia there is no minimum tax under the income tax structure, as such, but in most instances there are personal taxes.

RELATIVE TAX BURDENS

Table 3.2 shows the typical tax burden in the various countries and, for purposes of comparison, the United Kingdom and the United States. It must be kept in mind that the deductions vary, and thus the figures are by no means entirely comparable.

A few general observations can be made. Ghana has by far the lightest tax. For single persons, the taxes in Sierra Leone and in Southern Rhodesia and Nyasaland exceed those in the United Kingdom at the top levels; for married couples, the Sierra Leone tax is higher than that of the United Kingdom at the top levels. However, in the lower brackets, which contain most of the taxpayers, the highest taxes are those of Western, Northern, and Eastern Nigeria, while those of the Rhodesias are the lowest. Most of the taxes exceed those of the United States at a number of income levels.

PAYE

Withholding, or PAYE, is a relatively new phenomenon in these countries, and is now confined to Ghana and the four jurisdictions in Nigeria, plus the personal tax (not income tax) in Southern Rhodesia and Tanganyika.

In Ghana, commencing on July 1, 1962, every employer is required to deduct tax from each employee's wages on a monthly basis. Withholding is simplified by the absence of allowances except for the single £240 consolidated allowance. No tax is deducted if the wages are less than £20 a month. Persons gaining incomes solely from employment are not required to file annual tax returns. Each employer must keep a file card on each employee. When a person becomes unemployed, refunds of amounts previously paid during the year are granted. Persons other than employees are taxed on the basis of the past year rather than the current year; there is no declaration-of-estimated-income system. To speed up payment, however, traders are taxed initially on a presumptive basis on $7\frac{1}{2}\%$ of their turnover (that is, this amount is assumed to be taxable income), and subsequent adjustments are made when detailed examination of returns and accounts shows the correct amount of tax.

All four taxing jurisdictions in Nigeria require withholding. In

TABLE 3.2 RELATIVE INCOME TAX BURDENS, SELECTED INCOME LEVELS, TAX ROUNDED TO NEAREST POUND, FOR 1962 INCOMES

Income (pounds)	Sierra Leone	Ghana	Nigeria-Lagos	Western Nigeria	Northern Nigeria	Eastern Nigeria	East Africa	Northern Rhodesia	Southern Rhodesia and Nyasaland	United Kingdom	United States
Single Person											
500	5	4	10	18	16	28	28	6	8	49	47
1000	25	20	53	42	54	75	115	56	68	192	137
2000	205	86	258	227	202	286	363	244	292	493	341
3000	580	191	550	452	440	597	725	594	712	795	589
4000	1080	348	918	772	747	947	1169	955	1146	1097	880
5000	1580	544	1372	1192	1129	1372	1663	1342	1610	1440	1218
Married Couple, Two Children											
500	0	4	0	8	16	23	0	0	0	0	0
1000	10	20	28	28	54	60	10	0	0	0	9
2000	130	86	208	150	202	234	120	93	111	377	189
3000	455	191	484	382	440	506	435	340	408	678	377
4000	930	348	838	674	747	781	820	610	732	980	584
5000	1430	544	1269	1066	1129	1106	1275	997	1196	1324	841

Nigeria-Lagos, employers must withhold both the income tax and the income rate. But because of allowances, in order to obtain correct withholding, a coding system is established to inform the employer of the amount to deduct, the code number for each taxpayer being determined by the number of dependents and other allowances. Thus the tax liability for each year for employees is controlled by the income for that year and the dependency status of the previous year. So long as the person has no other income, no assessment is necessary at the end of the year (although the taxpayer may request it). If there was other income in the previous year, it is deducted from the personal allowance figure so that, in effect, tax on this amount is paid through withholding as well, but on a year-late basis. There is no exemption of employers by number of employees, but withholding is required only for employees whose compensation exceeds £300 a year; thus domestic help, etc., is in fact not covered. Persons other than employees are taxed in the usual fashion on the previous-year basis.

In Western Nigeria, withholding was introduced on April 1, 1961. Two sets of tables were established. For incomes up to £300, no allowances are provided, and the minimum tax rate is applied. On those above £300, taxpayers are coded, as in Lagos, on the basis of allowances. A return must be filed annually to indicate dependency and other factors influencing allowances, so that the employer may deduct the correct amounts. All employers are subject, although no tax is deducted on casual labor. Other taxpayers are assessed on the basis of the previous year's income.

Northern Nigeria introduced a PAYE system when it established its own income tax, effective April 1, 1962. As in the West, there are two schedules. A flat rate applies to persons with incomes under £400, without allowances; those with incomes in excess of £400 are subject to the regular graduated rates, after allowances. For the former group, a general-purpose card is prepared by the employer for each employee; for the second group a special card is prepared by the revenue division and supplied to the employer, indicating the amounts of allowances to be considered in making the deductions. Each employee is required to file a return at the end of the year, unlike the Eastern Nigeria and Lagos rule. In Northern Nigeria, currently, only those employers specified by the government are required (or permitted) to deduct. This group has been limited to the government and a few large companies; the intent is to extend the system slowly over the next several years. Initially there were about 30,000 employees and 300 employers covered.

The Eastern Nigeria government was one of the first in Africa to introduce PAYE. No attempt is made to apply the system to all employees, but only to those for whom the system is regarded as practicable; in 1962 there were about 1,800 employers, with 17,000 to 18,000 employees, subject. The employee notifies his employer directly of his family situation rather than via a return filed with the government. No return is required from the employee at the end of the year unless he has other income; the employer must file a statement of amounts paid to each employee. For casual workers, a franking machine comparable to a postage meter is used. The employer brings the cards into a tax office, pays the tax, and the machine imprints a record of payment onto the card. The card is transferred from one employer to another as the worker moves, and it is turned in at the end of the year. Normally withholding does not apply to nonwage income, which is taxed at the end of the year.

In Sierra Leone, East Africa, and Rhodesia consideration has been given to the use of PAYE for some time. In Sierra Leone and East Africa the governments and, on a voluntary basis, a few large employers do withhold, but not on a current basis; essentially, they merely collect the previous year's income tax from the employees by deductions from wages. The governments have been reluctant to introduce general withholding for two reasons: the inadequate staffs of the income tax departments, and the feeling that many employers cannot be relied upon to withhold. But currently the governments hope to move slowly toward withholding. In Rhodesia it is expected that a PAYE system will be introduced in the next few years.

One interesting case of PAYE is its use with the Southern Rhodesia personal tax, which, while not an income tax in the usual sense, is related in form. This practice is described in Chapter 5. When the employer has fewer than 12 employees, he must purchase stamps which he applies to a card kept for each employee; larger firms employ the usual return system. For the former group no return is required at the end of the year either from employer or worker; control is maintained by periodic house-to-house checks by inspectors of all households and business firms. It is estimated that in Bulawayo, a major commercial center, for example, 90% of all non-African households would be subject to the withholding requirement. A list of the return-filing employers is maintained, but not of the stamp-card employers. The system has gone into operation only in the last year, and is one of the few attempts anywhere in the world to subject all household employees to tax on a PAYE basis.

TIMING

Except for persons covered by PAYE, the taxes are characterized by an extremely long time lag between receipt of the income and payment of tax. With the Nigerian Federal (company and Lagos) taxes, in April of 1963, for example, returns were mailed for the year ending March 31 (with any period back to December 31 accepted).

Assessments are made during the ensuing months, and tax is payable in two installments: two months after the receipt of the assessment notice, and March 31, 1964, more than a year beyond the end of the tax year. In East Africa, which operates on a calendar year basis, the returns are mailed in January of the following year, and are due back in 30 days; in fact, only 40% are returned by June. Assessments cannot be made until after the tax rates are determined in the budgets (normally in May). Tax is payable: for individuals in two installments, October 31 and March 31; for companies, December 31. Ghana and Rhodesia have a substantially shorter cycle; in both these countries full payment is due 30 days after receipt of the assessment. These long time lags represent obvious deficiencies in the operation of the taxes, in terms of revenue and in relation to economic stabilization policies.

AVERAGING OF INCOME

Few countries in the world have seriously tackled the problem of irregular incomes beyond loss carry-over rules; East Africa is the only one in the group under study to attempt to do so. In East Africa when a person's income falls by more than 50% from one year to the next, he is permitted, subject to certain restrictions, to average the income of the two years. This is a rather crude form of averaging, but it does serve to minimize the difficulties for a taxpayer whose income has fallen sharply but who owes substantial tax on the previous year's income. If payment of the tax were placed on a current-year basis, there would be much less justification for this type of solution.

COMPANY TAXES

All of the countries impose separate company taxes. In Ghana, there is no integration of personal and company taxes. The latter applies to the entire net profit, with no adjustment on dividends at either the company or individual level. However, the personal income tax in Ghana is lower than is typical. In the other countries, complete integration of the personal and company taxes is provided, except for the corporation tax levied in East Africa in 1962 as a supplement to the company tax. The highest company tax rate is that of Sierra Leone (45%). The rates are 40% in Ghana, Nigeria, and Rhodesia ($33\frac{1}{3}\%$ Federation tax plus 20% supplement in each of the three regions), and $27\frac{1}{2}\%$ in East Africa, plus the 10% corporation tax.

However, in Ghana and Rhodesia adjustments are made for small companies, and in Nigeria for new companies (apart from pioneer companies legislation noted below). In Ghana, if the taxable income

47

is under £5,000, and the issued share capital is under £10,000, there is no tax the first two years of assessment and a 20% rate in the following years. If the earnings are under £5,000 but the share capital is over £10,000, the 20% rate applies from the beginning. If the income is between £5,000 and £10,000, the rate is 20% on the first £5,000, 25% on the next £2,000, 30% on the next £1,500, and 35% on the next £1,500. There are several restrictions relating to directors' salaries and foreign ownership.

In Rhodesia, on private companies—that is, ones owned by four or fewer persons—the rate is approximately $32\frac{1}{2}$% (including the surcharge) on the first £25,000 of income.

In Nigeria, tax on private companies is reduced during the first six years of their operation; if the profits do not exceed £1,000, there is full remission of tax the first year, two thirds for the next two years, and one third the next two years. If the earnings are between £1,000 and £3,000, the relief is less. There is no relief on profits above £3,000.

These rules, which are common in non-African countries as well, are of course designed to aid the growth of small new companies, which must expand largely from reinvested earnings. In Rhodesia the reduction was provided only in 1961; the government sought to aid investment and economic development without suffering a drastic loss in revenue, and was convinced that the tax reduction would be more significant for growth of the smaller companies than for larger ones.

Apart from these concessions to small companies, Sierra Leone, Ghana, and Nigeria grant so-called pioneer companies relief whereby, upon specific application, relief from income tax is provided, typically for five years, to new companies. This rule is of particular significance for foreign investors; an attempt is made to confine its use to new industrial investment which will make significant contributions to the development of the country. These programs have all been subject to administrative difficulties, and East Africa and Rhodesia have avoided them, largely for this reason. They are discussed at greater length in Chapter 9.

Reduced rates are provided in some instances for certain types of enterprises. Mining companies in East Africa are taxed at 20% instead of the basic $27\frac{1}{2}$% rate, and oil production companies are subject to a 50-50 profit-sharing arrangement in Nigeria in lieu of regular taxes. Special levies apply to diamond and iron ore producers in Sierra Leone.

THE UNDISTRIBUTED PROFITS PROBLEM

With top-level personal tax rates much higher than company rates, as in East Africa (75% *vs.* $37\frac{1}{2}$%), there is an inevitable tendency for the corporate form of organization to be used as a means to escape high-level personal taxes, a tendency aggravated by the failure to tax capital gains. In East Africa, under the 1952 Income Tax Management Act, if a private company failed to distribute at least 60% of the profits in any one year, the difference was assumed to have been distributed to the stockholders and was taxed to them. This provision did not work well in practice, primarily because numerous additional assessments against individuals were necessary, and complications arose with intercorporate stock ownership.

Accordingly, in 1958, a penalty tax was imposed on the company (rather than on the individual stockholders) of $47\frac{1}{2}\%$[4] if the company did not distribute at least 75% of its profit. But, to avoid interfering with expansion of companies by direct reinvestment of earnings, it is provided that companies can issue debentures to stockholders in lieu of cash payments; the stockholders pay tax on these as though they were cash income payments, and the company is free of penalty tax on undistributed profits. In practice, after initial complaints, the system has worked well, most companies distributing $67\frac{1}{2}\%$ or more of profits in order to escape penalty tax. In 1960 the penalty tax yielded only £59,000.

Rhodesia has a similar system. A company deducts from profits the taxes paid on the income, plus one third of total profits, plus all dividends paid, and is subject to undistributed profits tax on the remainder. The rate, however, is relatively low: $13\frac{3}{4}\%$ on the first £2,000 of undistributed profits, 25% on the remainder. The difference between the company rate and the top personal rate ($33\frac{1}{3}\%$ and 47%, without territorial surcharges) is much less than in East Africa. The other countries have not attempted to meet the undistributed profits problem.

COVERAGE OF THE TAXES

Unlike the income taxes of the United Kingdom and the United States, the taxes under consideration cover only a very small portion of the population, as shown in Table 3.3. The figures are only approximations, since the population figures of the countries are by no means accurate or up to date. By far the highest figure is to be found in Eastern Nigeria (apart from the income "rate" of Nigeria-Lagos). This situation, however, reflects the use of a minimum tax, which brings the income tax as such down to the lower income levels. In some other jurisdictions, as, for example, Northern Nigeria, persons in the lower levels are reached by separate personal taxes, which do not show up in the income tax totals. Apart from Nigeria,

---

[4] Applied to total income less the sum of $32\frac{1}{2}\%$ of income plus dividends paid.

TABLE 3.3   NUMBERS OF INCOME TAX PAYERS

Taxing Jurisdiction	Number of Individual Taxpayers	Number of Company Taxpayers	Individual Taxpayers as Percentage of Population
Rhodesia	74,328	4,553	0.9
East Africa:			
Over-all	85,993	4,417	0.4
Kenya	53,302	2,243	0.9
Tanganyika	18,266	633	0.2
Uganda	13,396	875	0.2
Zanzibar	1,671	22	0.5
Nigeria:		1,500	
Eastern Nigeria	1,119,000		13
Northern Nigeria	35,000		0.2
Lagos, Income Tax	26,700		8
Income Rate	120,000		33
Western Nigeria	n.a.		
Ghana	13,000*	*	0.3
Sierra Leone	13,000	250	0.6

Years: Rhodesia, 1960; East Africa, 1960–1961; Eastern Nigeria, 1958; Northern Nigeria, Lagos, and Ghana, estimates for 1962; Sierra Leone, 1961.
* Companies included in figure for individual taxpayers.

Kenya and Rhodesia, with nearly 1% coverage, have the highest figures, essentially because they have the highest numbers of Europeans. The figure for Southern Rhodesia alone is about 2%. Tanganyika, Uganda,[5] and Northern Nigeria have the lowest figures.

The extremely low figures reflect, of course, the relatively liberal personal allowances, and the very low per capita income of the bulk of the population. In East Africa and Rhodesia, there are extremely few African taxpayers, simply because of the low incomes; even in Ghana and Nigeria, most people are barely above the subsistence farming level.

References on income taxation are to be found at the end of Chapter 4.

[5] Africans were not subject to income tax in Uganda until 1962, and thus the percentage in the future will be greater. Uganda is the only East African country which, at the present, has any significant number of Africans with incomes high enough to be subject to the tax.

4 Income Taxation: Staff and Operations

ADMINISTRATIVE ORGANIZATION AND STAFFS

The organizational structure for operation of the income taxes in the various countries is similar and need not be reviewed in detail. The income taxes (plus in some instances other levies, but in no case including customs and excises) are under the jurisdiction of a Commissioner (in Nigeria-Federal and Western Nigeria, a board) appointed by the government on a nonpolitical basis. There is also an Assistant Commissioner; a small Investigation Branch; a staff of Inspectors or Assessing Officers, who do most of the work of ascertaining and assessing tax; and Tax Officers, whose exact functions vary but include assessment of uncomplicated returns, checking on delinquents, and the like.

A few examples will indicate the size and scope of the staffs. In Ghana, in addition to the Commissioner and Assistant Commissioner, there are 3 senior inspectors, 9 inspectors, 11 junior inspectors, and 40 "special officers" who are essentially tax policemen. Eastern Nigeria has from 40 to 45 inspectors. In East Africa, in addition to the usual top echelon, there are 2 assistant deputy commissioners, 9 regional commissioners, 34 assistant commissioners (equivalent roughly to senior inspectors in other areas), 49 assessors, 116 tax officers. In Rhodesia, in addition to top personnel, there are 4 senior inspectors, 10 inspectors, 18 grade one assessors, and 110 assessors, tax officers, and tax clerks.

Salary Scales

Because of different classifications, precise comparison of salary scales is not easy. Table 4.1 gives a rough comparison. Rhodesia,

TABLE 4.1 SALARY SCALES, INCOME TAX STAFFS

	Annual Salary in Pounds			
	Sierra Leone	Ghana	Nigeria-Federal	Rhodesia
Tax Officer	—	—	—	850
Junior Inspector		680–980	720–1,260	
Inspector	684	1,040–1,320		1,300–1,800*
Senior Inspector	1,467	1,470–1,570	1,314–1,584	

* Designated as Assessing Officers. The term "Inspector" in Rhodesia is used for more senior personnel.

particularly, stresses the inadequacy of the present scale in attracting competent personnel.

Educational Requirements and Training

The general aim of the tax administrators is to obtain university graduates, preferably in accounting, so far as possible, for inspector ranks. Ghana appears to be the most successful in accomplishing this goal. All governments, and particularly the regional governments of Nigeria, are forced in part to rely upon persons who are taken on after completing secondary school, serve as tax officers, and are gradually trained for assessing and investigatory work. In the past there was substantial recruitment of inspectors from the United Kingdom, either on a permanent basis, particularly in East Africa and Rhodesia, or from Inland Revenue on a temporary basis. This practice has come to a complete end in Ghana (which is in the best position to supply its own needs) and is gradually declining in other jurisdictions.

East Africa and Rhodesia, with their relatively complicated taxes, are finding great difficulty in filling positions and maintaining staffs. Because of political uncertainties, people are reluctant to come to these countries on a permanent basis, and the East African administration is under great pressure to Africanize as rapidly as possible. But, unfortunately, in East Africa, unlike Ghana, there are only a very limited number of Africans with the training needed for the positions, and they are in great demand for more attractive and rewarding jobs. Rhodesia, which recruits largely from the United Kingdom and South Africa, is now finding it almost impossible to obtain people from these areas; its own supply of university graduates or others with adequate education is extremely limited.

The extent of Africanization of the income tax services varies widely. In Ghana it is complete, from the Commissioner level down. In Sierra Leone the inspectors are African, but the top personnel remain British, pending training of additional Sierra Leonians. In Nigeria, the Western Nigeria government has carried Africanization furthest, including the position of regional tax administrator. In Eastern Nigeria the process has been carried almost as far, but the Commissioner is not African. In Northern Nigeria, which has relatively fewer trained Africans than the other regions, the top personnel are European, and two inspectors are on loan from the United Kingdom to train African inspectors. The Nigerian Federal government makes substantial use of European senior inspectors but is moving toward Africanization.

East Africa and Rhodesia have, as yet, primarily European staffs. East Africa in 1961 had 24 men on loan from the Board of Inland Revenue; but they were scheduled to return to England in 1963. There are no Africans in assessing or higher positions, although attempts are being made, in conjunction with the Royal College in Nairobi, to train Africans for this work. A similar situation prevails in Rhodesia, but less attempt has been made to attract Africans.

Training Programs

Two general procedures have been followed with respect to training. Several of the countries have sent junior officers to the United Kingdom for the course provided by the Overseas Tax Office and available in the future under the technical assistance scheme. The other approach is the use of an internal training program, as in Nigeria-Federal, East Africa, and Rhodesia. Typically, this is a two-year program, involving part-time work and part-time instruction. Smaller countries, such as Sierra Leone, find this approach more difficult. Cooperative arrangements have been made in Kenya, and in Ghana, for cooperation with the universities, and in the case of Ghana with the Institute of Public Administration.

Centralization

All of the taxing jurisdictions except Sierra Leone employ a substantial degree of decentralization in the operation of the system, using divisional offices which are autonomous so far as handling of returns, making assessments, and collections are concerned. To headquarters is assigned general policy decision-making, interpretations, statistical work, and investigation work. Ghana has district offices in Accra (two), Kumasi, Takoradi, and Koforidua; Nigeria-Federal in Kano, Jos, and Lagos; Northern Nigeria in Jos and Kano; East Africa a total of 11; Rhodesia 10. There are 27 divisional offices in Eastern Nigeria. The general practice is to limit an office in terms of numbers of accounts, and thus to have more than one division in the larger cities; this is true in Accra, Nairobi, and Salisbury, for example. Such a procedure would be less necessary and perhaps undesirable if greater use were made of data-processing equipment.

INCOME TAX PROCEDURE

The taxing jurisdictions included in the study have based their procedure primarily upon that of the United Kingdom (with some South African influence in Rhodesia). The general procedures will be noted, with reference to major exceptions in particular countries.

Taxpayer Rolls

In Sierra Leone, Ghana, and the Nigerian Federal government, together with Western, Northern, and Eastern Nigeria for larger taxpayers, ledger lists of taxpayers serve as the basis for mailing returns, recording assessments and payments, and ascertainment of delinquents by visual review. East Africa uses cards arranged in numerical order as a basis for preparing returns for mailing, and Burroughs ledger cards for recording assessments and payments. In each country, a manila folder file is kept for each taxpayer; usually these are grouped into three classes: employees, companies, and all others, frequently referred to as traders. Different colors are used for each group. A master alpha file of taxpayers' names and numbers is also typically employed.

However, with the Nigeria taxes which have minimum levies and thus cover virtually all families, no roll is kept for the smaller taxpayers, as explained in Chapter 5.

Assessments

Typically, the taxpayers have 30 to 40 days to send the returns in. Following British tradition, in no instance does the taxpayer calculate his own tax. This is done by the assessing officer. Only Rhodesia has evidenced any interest in self-assessment, but is somewhat reluctant to attempt it.

The assessments are made by officials known generally as Inspectors in West Africa, and as Assessing Officers in East Africa and Rhodesia. In East Africa, however, the relatively simple employee assessments are made by the Tax Officers, a more junior rank of employee. In making the assessment, information returns supplied by employers are checked, and, with traders, the profit-and-loss statements and balance sheets, which are filed with the returns. Frequently the inspector will require additional information from the taxpayer, or asks the latter to bring in his books and records. As a universal practice, the inspector will not go to the taxpayer's place of business.

The taxes on the lower income groups in Eastern and Western Nigeria are assessed by local assessment committees, as explained in Chapter 5.

In Nigeria-Federal, assessments are submitted to a Committee of Scrutineers, made up of businessmen familiar with the particular type of business activity, for review.

Collection

Collection is normally separated from assessment. Payments are typically made by the taxpayer by check (except for the lower-income taxpayers in Nigeria). The payment is recorded in the ledger or on the ledger card. After a certain period, visual check is made of the ledger or ledger card, delinquents ascertained, and notices sent out. Ultimately legal action to compel payment is made if voluntary payment is not forthcoming.

In Eastern Nigeria and Western Nigeria, apart from PAYE, collection is in the hands of locally appointed collectors (appointed by the chiefs or local councils). In the east there are some 13,000 collectors. They receive a percentage (6% in the east) of the amounts collected. In Northern Nigeria collection is in the hands of the Native Authorities (except for employees subject to PAYE and the Europeans). This policy is a result of the desire to maintain the prestige of these authorities, and relatively high standards of administration are found.

Enforcement

There are four major elements of enforcement policy:

1. Attainment of complete taxpayer rolls. The names of all taxpayers must be listed on the rolls. The countries have not developed highly systematic procedures for accomplishing this result, although leakage is not likely to be very great. Major methods include check of business and motor vehicle licenses, property sales, contracts awarded, and block-by-block check of traders.

The portions of the Nigerian (Eastern, Western, and Lagos) taxes on the lower income groups, for which no rolls are kept and no returns are required, involve substantially different procedures; these are discussed in Chapter 5.

2. Obtaining returns. All jurisdictions report some failure of taxpayers to file their returns. East Africa does not send a reminder, and finds that nearly half of the returns do not come in on schedule. An assessment is made on the basis of the previous year's returns

and sent to the taxpayer, and if no payment is forthcoming, usual collection measures are undertaken. Elsewhere, the usual rule is to add a penalty (5%, for example, in Ghana), and to send a reminder. If the return is not forthcoming, an assessment is made. The tendency is to seek to make a reasonable assessment, or one likely to be slightly above the actual figure. However, at least one country is reported to make an assessment well above the figure believed to be correct.

3. Accuracy of assessments. In making assessments, the greatest difficulty arises with smaller business firms, whose records leave much to be desired. The precise problems vary with the country. In Ghana and Nigeria, for example, the "mammies" who handle much of the retail trade and often have substantial incomes keep few or no records and are particularly hostile to taxation. In parts of West Africa much of the retailing above the level of market stalls is handled by Lebanese; in East Africa most business is in the hands of Indians. Records, frequently inadequate, are often kept in languages other than English or the African language of the area. Assessments must often be based on external criteria such as rentals paid, living patterns, increases in wealth of the owners, and other somewhat arbitrary factors. Unfortunately, many of the governments lack adequate numbers of trained and experienced inspectors who are competent to make high-quality assessments on this basis.

Apart from the assessment section, the larger countries maintain some form of investigative branch, which makes detailed investigations of taxpayers when the inspectors suspect deliberate fraud or substantial evasion. The investigation staffs are small: there is one investigator in Ghana, for example, and two in the Nigerian Federal tax administration. These persons are usually chartered accountants or the equivalent. Unlike an inspector, an investigator will typically visit the taxpayer's place of business and review all records. In some instances, particularly in Rhodesia, the records may be seized and taken to the revenue office.

4. Obtaining payment. The final problem is that of enforcing payment, which is due either a certain number of days after the assessment is mailed or on a certain date. The procedure is more or less standard: a percentage penalty is applied, and a notice sent. If this action does not bring results, suit is filed to force payment.

It is very difficult to evaluate the over-all efficiency of income tax administration in these countries. The inadequate record-keeping on the part of small shopkeepers is a major limitation; on the other hand, most farmers and many small shopkeepers are below the personal allowance figure, and thus problems of enforcement do not arise. In the past, the taxes have applied primarily to Europeans in most of these countries; as more and more non-Europeans, with initially lower levels of education and traditions of record keeping, become subject, the task of enforcement may well become more difficult. East African countries (except Zanzibar) supplement their general enforcement program by a requirement for tax clearance before a person can leave the country.

Data-Processing Equipment

The African countries have lagged somewhat in the introduction of data-processing equipment in tax administration, although all are aware of the possibilities. Introduction of such equipment has been retarded by the relatively small number of accounts, by the difficulties of obtaining an adequate number of trained people for the maintenance of the equipment, and by other considerations. Sierra Leone, Ghana, the Nigerian Federal government, Eastern Nigeria, and Northern Nigeria have at the moment no such equipment at all so far as internal operation of the tax is concerned. In Ghana a card is punched for each account (from a special book in which returns are recorded), but it is turned over to the Government Statistician's office for statistical purposes only. Both Ghana and the Nigerian Federal government, however, are now in the process of considering introduction of extensive data-processing equipment. The Sierra Leone administration believes the use of machinery to be unwarranted at present. The Northern Nigeria government considered the use of data-processing equipment from the time of introduction of the tax in 1962, but concluded that its use was not warranted for the first five or six years of the tax. The decentralized nature of the administration in Western Nigeria virtually precludes the use of such equipment.

The three jurisdictions which make some use of equipment are Eastern Nigeria, East Africa (which once made much greater use), and Rhodesia. Eastern Nigeria uses an elaborate punch card system for internal balancing and statistical purposes, and publishes extensive statistical reports relating to tax payments which are not possible in the other Nigerian jurisdictions. East Africa uses Burroughs bookkeeping machines for posting to ledger cards and balancing. For some years prior to 1961 it used Powers Samas punch card equipment for posting and ascertainment of delinquency, as well as for statistics and balancing. The system was abandoned for a variety of reasons: the equipment was old and needed replacing; certain activities of the Common Services Organization, which had also utilized the equipment, were transferred back to the territorial governments; and the administration regarded the introduction of a visible ledger card (which, however, can be produced with most types of punch card equipment) as essential for operation of the tax. The abandonment of the equipment has nevertheless reduced the efficiency of operations in certain aspects and may in the long run prove to be a mistake.

The Rhodesia Federation government uses National Cash Register bookkeeping equipment for posting and balancing and has begun to experiment with use of an electronic computer; in 1962 one belonging to the Southern Rhodesia government was used in the preparation of assessments. As of 1962 until the present this was card-operated, but shift to tape equipment is contemplated in the near future.

THE FUTURE OF AFRICAN INCOME TAXATION

The basic question which has been under discussion in all of the countries of the study is: With increased difficulty of maintaining staff as the supply of European personnel is cut off, and as more and more Africans rise into income levels such that they will become subject to tax, will it be possible to continue the operation of the relatively complex types of taxes now in use, with numerous allowances and other features? The first country to make a drastic change was Ghana when, in 1961, it abandoned the traditional British type of tax in favor of one with a single consolidated allowance and no personal deductions of any kind, in conjunction with the establishment of withholding. Northern Nigeria, in establishing its tax in 1962, provided likewise for a single consolidated allowance, almost a necessity in this predominately Moslem country, but did authorize allowances of a character which will primarily affect the higher income groups. In the other Nigerian jurisdictions, there has been less consideration of simplification, and the basic Income Tax Management Act of 1961 provides for a relatively complicated over-all structure.

Greatest attention has been given to the question in East Africa, which is faced with a drastic loss in key personnel consequent to independence of the constituent countries. The four governments and the income tax administration have pursued this question at great length, and, in 1961, drastic elimination of allowances was effected, plus other changes such as the ending of tax on owner-occupied homes, in an effort to make the tax simpler. Rhodesia, likewise faced with serious personnel shortages for somewhat different reasons, is reviewing simplification.

To the outside observer, it would appear that the traditional colonial income tax, modeled on the United Kingdom tax, and originally intended primarily for Europeans in the African countries, is unnecessarily complicated, as compared, for example, to the United States tax, for the African environment. Simplified returns, alternate standard deductions, like those of the United States, and other measures to make the task of filing and checking returns easier should greatly simplify administration. It should be possible, however, to adjust the tax to some degree in terms of numbers of dependents, with a limit on the number, without materially complicating the operating of the levy.

Apart from the question of simplification is that of general attacks on income taxation on the grounds that it is detrimental to economic development. This point of view was expressed by representations to the East African Commission of Inquiry on Income Tax,[1] by speeches by officials of the Rockefeller Brothers Fund in Nigeria, and in the *Memorandum* submitted by the Buganda government to the Fiscal Commission of Uganda,[2] to mention only a few examples. But the governments generally accept the position that an income tax, even though as yet affecting only a small percentage of the population (except in Nigeria), constitutes a necessary step in the direction of making the tax structure more equitable and evident to the taxpayer, and that at existing rates it does not have significant effect in retarding development.

The general question of the role of the income tax in developing economies will be considered in Chapter 9.

SELECTED REFERENCES, CHAPTERS 3 AND 4

Orewa, G. Oka, *Taxation in Western Nigeria*. Oxford: Oxford University Press for the Nigerian Institute of Social and Economic Research, 1962.
Report of the East African Commission of Inquiry on Income Tax. Nairobi: High Commission Printer, 1957.

Ghana, *Income Tax Ordinance*, 1943, and amendments.
East African Income Tax Management Act, 1958, and amendments.
Nigeria, *Income Tax Management Act*, 1961.
Northern Nigeria, *Personal Tax Law*, 1962.
Western Nigeria, *Income Tax Law*, 1957
Eastern Nigeria, *Finance Law*, 1962.
Government of Western Nigeria, *Explanatory Notes about Personal Income Tax in Western Nigeria*, 1961.

[1] *Report of the East African Commission of Inquiry on Income Tax* (Nairobi: High Commission Printer, 1957).

[2] *Memorandum Prepared by the Treasury of H.H. The Kabaka's Government of Buganda for the Fiscal Commission appointed by H.E. the Governor of Uganda* (Kampala: 1962).

Ministry of Finance, Northern Nigeria, *Personal Tax*, 1962.

Internal Revenue Division, Eastern Nigeria, *Annual Report*.

Federation of Rhodesia and Nyasaland, *Income Tax Act*, 1954, as amended.

Annual Report, Commissioner of Taxes, Federation of Rhodesia and Nyasaland.

Andic, F. and S., "A Survey of Ghana's Tax System and Finances." *Public Finance*, Vol. 13 (#1, 1963), pp. 5–44.

5 The Personal Tax[1]

A CHARACTERISTIC FEATURE of the tax systems of the eight countries is the universal use, except in Zanzibar, of a very simplified form of direct personal tax which is in a sense hybrid between a poll tax and an elementary form of income tax. The names differ among the countries, with the terms "general tax," "community tax," "personal tax," and "income rate" being employed. The term "personal tax" will be used in this study. The taxes differ somewhat in their structure. But they are basically very similar, with the following major features:

1. Application of a minimum tax to all persons (more specifically, in most instances, to all adult males), except a small number of disabled, elderly, or destitute persons exempted by administrative discretion.

2. Use, in most of the taxes, of a limited degree of graduation, which stops at a relatively low figure. Some jurisdictions still em-

[1] For material in this chapter, the author is particularly indebted to the officials of H.H. the Kabaka's government of Buganda for their cooperation in explaining detailed operation of the tax. Attention is called to the significant work by U. K. Hicks, *Development from Below* (Oxford: Oxford University Press, 1961), for a general discussion of African local government and finance, with reference to the development of the personal tax systems. A portion of the material in this chapter appeared in the December, 1962, issue of the *National Tax Journal*, and is used by permission of the National Tax Association.

ploy a flat rate, but the tendency, particularly in the last ten years, is toward greater use of progression. Rates are fixed amounts per bracket of income rather than percentages.

3. Assessment of tax primarily without the use of returns, by direct assessment by local committees of laymen, rather than professional tax officers.

4. The absence of allowances and deductions.

5. Particularly in rural areas, assessment in part on the basis of external criteria of income and wealth, rather than on any careful effort to ascertain actual income, which is, in fact, virtually impossible under the circumstances, given the levels of education and record keeping.

These taxes all developed from hut or poll taxes imposed at uniform rates by the central governments under the British colonial administrations, dating back in some countries for half a century. The oldest of the systems, that of Northern Nigeria, actually predates British rule, originating under the regime of the Fulani Emirs in the last century, and modified and continued by Lord Lugard. The poll taxes were designed to place some tax burden directly on the Africans, as a means of increasing their sense of responsibility for government services, and to avoid complete reliance on customs duties, the other prime source of colonial revenues. In part, at least in some instances, particularly in Southern Rhodesia, there was the added motive of seeking to encourage Africans to enter the commercial sector of the economy by selling a portion of their produce or hiring out their services, rather than relying entirely on subsistence farming.

USE AND REVENUE IMPORTANCE

Initially the taxes were imposed as uniform-rate poll or hut taxes (the latter were sometimes preferred because huts were easier to find than people), but the obvious deficiencies of the poll tax in terms of both revenue and equity led to the gradual introduction of graduation. Likewise, they were initially central government levies. The tendency has been to shift them to the local governments, but they are still also widely employed by the central governments.

Central versus Local Government Use

As the situation stands, as of 1963, the personal tax is levied as follows:

1. Local governments only: Sierra Leone; Ghana; Uganda (central government tax expired December 31, 1962); plus Lagos, whose tax is operated by the Nigerian Federal government.

2. Central government only: Southern Rhodesia; Northern Nigeria (with local administration); Western Nigeria (plus flat-rate local levies for specific purposes); Nyasaland (plus special flat-rate local education tax).

3. Both local and central: Kenya, Tanganyika, Eastern Nigeria, Northern Rhodesia.

Relation to the Income Tax

In Eastern and Western Nigeria, the taxes are imposed as a portion of the income tax structure, the income tax law providing for a minimum rate, and the portion of the tax on the lower income levels being operated in the same manner as those personal taxes imposed separately. In the other jurisdictions in which the tax is used, a separate income tax is imposed, but with sufficiently high personal allowances that only a small percentage of the population, primarily non-African, is subject to it.

Persons subject to income tax also pay personal tax, with two exceptions. In Northern Nigeria, a person paying income tax is exempt from personal tax. In Nyasaland, the personal tax constitutes a credit against income tax liability for the Nyasaland surcharge to the Federation tax.

Revenue Importance

The personal taxes are significant but not major elements in the tax structures of the central governments which impose them, as shown in Table 5.1, for 1961–1962.

TABLE 5.1   PERCENTAGE YIELD OF MAJOR TAXES,
JURISDICTIONS USING PERSONAL TAX

	Northern Nigeria	Southern Rhodesia	Northern Rhodesia	Nyasaland	Kenya	Tanganyika
Personal Tax	14	13	3	25	6	6
Income Tax	5	44	90	64	38	25
Customs and Excises	27	24	2	6	46	64
Export Duties	46	—	—	—	—	—
Miscellaneous	8	19	5	5	10	5

Thus the personal tax exceeds the yield of the income tax in Northern Nigeria, yields one fourth of Nyasaland's revenue, and 13% in Southern Rhodesia.

In Uganda this tax is the chief tax source of the districts. In Buganda, for example, it raises 97% of the tax revenue collected by the Kingdom, and 47% of total government revenue (1961–1962). In 1959 the tax raised 61% of total government revenue in Bugisu, 54% in Teso, 42% in Ankole, and 34% in Busoga. In Kenya (1961) the tax yields 57% of the revenue of the African District Councils and 20% of their total revenue. In Tanganyika the tax yields 83% of the tax revenue of the local governments, and in Northern Nigeria, 86%. If the *jangali*, the cattle tax used in lieu of the community tax for the nomadic tribes, is added, the two together yield virtually the entire tax revenue. In Ghana the tax provided, in 1957 (the last year for which data are compiled), 82% of the tax revenue of the local councils and 33% of their total revenue.

Rate Structure

Flat rates are still employed in the local personal taxes of Eastern Nigeria, Sierra Leone, Ghana, Kenya (called "rates"), Tanganyika, and in both central and local personal taxes in Northern Rhodesia, and the central tax in Nyasaland. There are also flat-rate local taxes for special purposes in Western Nigeria and Nyasaland. The question of graduation has been under discussion in most of these jurisdictions. In Kenya, there is a strong belief on the part of various officials responsible for local government that the taxes should be graduated; so far, the Ministry of Finance has opposed this on the basis that only the Kenya government should use graduated taxation. A change in policy in the immediate future is not impossible. In Tanganyika, on the other hand, the law permits rural District Councils (formerly called Native Authorities) to impose either flat-rate or graduated personal taxes (or taxes on the site value of land, or on earnings and possessions), and the central government has encouraged the use of graduated rates. However, the flat-rate system remains almost universal; only Moshi, of the larger jurisdictions, has introduced graduation. The local areas prefer the flat-rate system because of avoidance of the problem of assessment.

In Northern Rhodesia, both central and local poll taxes have flat rates; under a general review now being made of the financial relations of central and local governments, there is some discussion of a single graduated personal tax. Nyasaland has a simple uniform poll tax, but with a much higher rate for Europeans than for Africans. Flat-rate (usually 5s.) education taxes are levied by certain District Councils.

The other jurisdictions in which flat rates are used are Sierra

Leone and Ghana; in both instances the tax is employed only at the local government level.[2] The evils of the flat rate are recognized in Sierra Leone, but the standards of local administration are typically less advanced than in much of Africa, and the government is not yet willing to shift to a graduated basis. By contrast, in Ghana, with its generally high level of administration compared to that in other West African countries, the central government has attempted to push the use of graduated rates (which are authorized by law), but with little success outside of a few jurisdictions in the far north. The municipalities and local councils are most unwilling to shift from the flat-rate system. Ghana was one of the last African countries in which any form of direct tax was introduced, because of a long-standing hostility toward this form of levy on the part of the two major groups, the coastal Fanti and the Ashanti of the interior. Eastern Nigeria local units can use graduated rates but do not do so.

Table 5.2 shows the structure of the flat-rate taxes; these taxes vary with different geographic areas, except with the Nyasaland tax, which is the same throughout the country but is much higher for

TABLE 5.2 FLAT-RATE PERSONAL TAXES

Country	Rate of Tax (range when rates vary geographically)
Sierra Leone, Local	25s.–30s.
Ghana, Local	8s.–80s.
Kenya, Local	50s.–60s.
Tanganyika, Local	20s.–60s.
Nyasaland, Central	30s.; Europeans, 160s.
Northern Rhodesia, Central	12/6–25s.
Northern Rhodesia, Local	7s.–30s.
Eastern Nigeria, Local	20s. (typical)

Europeans than for Africans. The lowest rates are the 8s. rates in some of the Ghana cities. A 20s. to 30s. rate is more common; the 50s. to 60s. rate of Kenya is one of the top ones, while the highest is the 80s. rate in some Ghana areas.[3]

Graduated Taxes

The graduated form of personal tax is of particular interest because of its hybrid nature between poll and income taxes and its likely increase in importance in the future.

[2] Sierra Leone's tax, originally levied as a central government hut tax, dates back to 1898. From 1911 to 1954 the tax remained at 5s.; in 1937 a 4s. local tax was added. Eventually the tax became exclusively a local levy, with a maximum rate of 25s. set after the tax riots of 1955.

[3] The currencies of all the countries involved are at par with the United Kingdom pound.

As noted, in Eastern and Western Nigeria the income tax structure itself extends down to the lowest income levels. In the east, the minimum rate of 27/6 applies to incomes up to £60, with steady graduation above, the rate brackets being only £10 wide. The effective rates are relatively high compared to most of the juris-dictions, 6.87% up to £700 income.[4] In Western Nigeria the minimum tax is also 27/6 (based on the presumption that everyone has at least £50 income) and a 3.75% rate above £50, up to £400; this is the only one of the taxes under consideration that has a percentage rate.[5] The Nigeria-Lagos tax, introduced in 1961, pro-vides a tax of 10s. on incomes up to £100, £1 on incomes from £101 to £200, and £3 on incomes in excess of £203, with intermediate rates on incomes between £200 and £203 to prevent marginal rates in excess of 100% in this range. Prior to 1961 the Lagos income tax had extended downward to include the lowest income groups, with a minimum of 7s.; the income tax now has an exemption of £300.

The Southern Rhodesia system likewise involves only a limited degree of progression.[6] The rate regarded as basic is 240s., assessed against all taxpayers except: (1) employees with incomes under £600 a year; (2) other persons applying for reduced tax on the basis of incomes less than £600; (3) persons living in designated African areas, subject to a rate of 40s. Those in the first two groups are assessed at 40s. if the income is under £300, and 120s. if the income is from £300 to £600.

The Tanganyika tax, since 1961,[7] exempts those with income under £100, and is the first of these taxes to provide a statutory exemption for adult males by amount of income. Previously, the minimum tax was 12s. The change was made to reduce the burden on the lowest income groups, to satisfy political demands for lessen-ing direct taxation, and to avoid administrative problems involved in collecting tax from large numbers of small taxpayers. The rates for 1962 are shown in Table 5.3.

[4] Direct taxation was introduced at a relatively recent date, in the late 1920's, in Eastern Nigeria, primarily at the local level. In 1956, the Eastern Nigeria government took over most of the direct taxing powers of the local governments and established the present income tax largely to finance universal education.

[5] The Western Nigeria income tax was extended to the lowest income levels in 1960, replacing the graduated local general income "rates" which had previously applied to incomes below £300. These dated back to 1918.

[6] This levy replaced the native tax as of July 1, 1961. The native tax consisted of a flat £2 rate on all adult African males; it dated back to the turn of the cen-tury, having been devised mainly to force more Africans to seek work on European-owned farms.

[7] Tanganyika replaced its house and poll tax by the graduated tax in 1953; previously only non-Africans had been subject to a graduated tax. Native Authorities were authorized to impose graduated taxes as early as 1942 but did not do so.

TABLE 5.3   SCHEDULE OF TANGANYIKA TAX RATES, 1962

Income (pounds)	Tax (shillings)	Tax as Percentage of Income, Lower End of Bracket
100–150	20	1
150–200	40	1.3
200–250	60	1.5
250–300	90	1.8
300–400	180	3
400–500	250	3.1
500–600	350	3.5
Over 600	450	3.75

The Uganda schedules are in all cases graduated but are not identical in the various districts.[8] The most important is the Buganda tax shown in Table 5.4.

TABLE 5.4   SCHEDULE OF BUGANDA TAX RATES, 1962

Income (pounds)	Tax (shillings)	Tax as Percentage of Income, Lower End of Bracket
Up to 48	40	—
48–90	60	6.25
90–180	100	5.6
180–300	150	4.2
300–420	200	3.3
420–540	300	3.6
540–660	400	3.7
660–720	500	3.8
Over 720	600	4.2

These rates are not progressive throughout, as in Tanganyika, the first bracket constituting 4.2% of income at the top of the bracket, the fourth bracket 2.5%, the seventh bracket 3.3%. In other districts of Uganda, as of 1959–1960, the minimum rates ranged from 22s. to 40s.; the top rate was 400s., the maximum allowed by the Uganda government. But several of the authorities ran their rates only up to 150s. The maximum allowed, as of 1962, was 600s.

[8] The graduated form of tax was first introduced in Uganda in 1954, replacing the African Authority poll tax which dated back to 1939. The change was designed mainly to increase the revenue potential. The flat-rate education tax was integrated into the personal tax in 1958. The Protectorate continued to use a 6s. poll tax until the end of 1962.

The rates of the Kenya tax,[9] as of 1962, are shown in Table 5.5. Later in 1962 those who earned under £120 were freed from paying the tax.

TABLE 5.5 SCHEDULE OF KENYA TAX RATES, 1963

Income (pounds)	Tax (shillings)	Tax as Percentage of Income, Lower End of Bracket
Less than 120	0	—
120–160	45	1.87
160–200	100	3.1
200–400	150	3.75
Over 400	200	2.5

The final graduated tax is that of Northern Nigeria, the one instance in which a person subject to income tax does not pay personal tax, £400 being the breaking point. Each Native Authority determines the total tax to be collected, and then ascertains the share to be collected in total by each district by a formula, which involves multiplying a certain rate by the adult male population of the district. The rates used, however, are greater in the wealthier districts than in the poorer ones; they range currently from 32s. to 55s.

In turn, the district total is allocated to each village on a population basis, and then rates on individuals in the village are established at such a level as to provide the requisite sum. These rates on individuals are graduated, except in certain districts in the southern part of the region. The usual practice is to place the bulk of the population in a minimum-rate group (with rates ranging from

---

[9] A brief survey of the history of the Kenya tax shows the extensive change which has occurred:

1933–1936: Graduated poll tax, based on income, minimum 30s., maximum 10,000s. (no income tax in this period).

1937–1939: Poll tax, nonnatives only: Europeans, 40s.; Asians, 30s.; Arabs and Somalis, 20s.

1940: Same structure; rates 60, 45, and 30s., respectively.

1941–1954: Personal tax, graduated, on all nonnatives: income under £60, 20s.; £60–120, 40s.; over £120, 60s.

1955–1957: Same structure; rates 40s. and 80s. in first two brackets; 120s. on income from £120 to £200; 200s. on income over £200.

1958–1959: Graduated personal tax on all races; rates: income under £120, 25s.; £120–160, 50s.; £160–200, 100s.; over £200, 150s.

1960–1961: Same structure; rates 20s., 45s., 100s., 150s., respectively.

1961–1963: Same structure; rates as in Table 5.5. First bracket tax eliminated in 1962.

During the period prior to 1958 there was also a flat-rate African poll tax.

10s. up to 60s). The remaining persons comprise a "wealthy" list, with a rough sort of graduation of tax.

Two major peculiarities of these rate structures should be noted. First, except in Nigeria, they produce marginal rates well over 100%; that is, as a person moves from one bracket to another, the tax rises much more than the income, thus providing an incentive not to gain the added income. Second, the effective rates, as percentages, vary within each bracket in a regressive fashion. This is an inevitable result of the application of given sums of tax to a range of incomes. In some instances the rates among brackets are also somewhat regressive; the Tanganyika tax is, however, progressive.

The various jurisdictions using graduated rates vary in the extent to which they actually attempt to ascertain income. As will be seen below in the discussion of assessment, the attempts are often very crude. But at least in terms of the law, the tax is directly related to income in the four Nigerian areas, Kenya, and Tanganyika (which defines income more precisely than the others), and Southern Rhodesia with respect to employees. For traders and commercial farming operations, business expenses are usually deductible; for the typical small farmer, they are usually not. Personal deductions and allowances are unknown except in a few Uganda districts; Teso permits allowances for certain dependents, and for school fees, for example.

The Significance of the Rates Relative to Income

As noted, for the lowest tax group, into which most of the population falls, the typical rates range from 10 to 40s., with a few, such as in Kenya, substantially higher. If Uganda is used as a basis for comparison, the estimated cash income per head is about 200s., or at least 800s. for the average family; the combined cash and subsistence income per head is 340s., or at least 1,360s. per family (in the narrow sense of that term).[10] Thus the minimum 40s. rate would constitute 5% of the family cash income. Those in the lowest income group would, of course, average less than the 800s. figure, but not a great deal less, because the great bulk of the population falls into this category. However, regional differences are great; in Kigezi (in the far southwest) the cash income is only 58s. per head, or perhaps 232s. per family; and thus the minimum 40s. tax represents a very high percentage of the income.

A study of the relationship of total personal tax collections to total personal income, less subsistence income, in Uganda for 1959 showed a range from 8.99% in Ankole, 8.83% in Kigezi, and 7.54%

[10] International Bank for Reconstruction and Development, *The Economic Development of Uganda* (Entebbe: Government Printer, 1961), Table S5.

in Bugisu to 2.6% in Buganda;[11] in other words, the high-income areas are imposing a much smaller relative burden than the poorer areas.

Other Aspects of Coverage

Initially the taxes applied only to men, presumably because the African woman did not usually earn an income as such (except in Ghana and parts of southern Nigeria, where for generations the women have conducted much of the retail trade). This rule remains today in Sierra Leone, Uganda (except for women owning land), Kenya (except for single women with income in excess of £60),[12] Northern Rhodesia, Nyasaland, Northern Nigeria, and for the Tanganyika local taxes with minor exceptions. Also, in effect, the tax does not apply to women at the lower levels in Eastern and Western Nigeria because of higher exemptions provided for women (£300 in the West, £100 in the East); in Eastern Nigeria women are completely exempt except for employees with incomes in excess of £100, and traders in six urban areas.

The break with tradition has been made, however, in several jurisdictions, and this trend is likely to continue. Ghana taxes women, although only at one half the usual rate. Tanganyika taxes single women only, married women being required to combine their incomes with those of their husbands. Southern Rhodesia applies the tax to all single women, but only to those married women who are employees. Only Lagos, after the change made in 1961, treats men and women in exactly the same fashion, as individual taxpayers. However, those women who have no incomes of their own are not in fact subject to tax. When women were added to the tax rolls in Lagos in 1961, near riots were created as numbers of market women marched on the Government House. Nevertheless, the tax remains applicable to them.

When the taxes were introduced, they were applied only to Africans. In time, special poll taxes of various kinds were imposed on non-Africans for education and other purposes. In recent years, with the general trend to eliminate all racial distinctions, most countries have consolidated their personal levies into single uniform personal taxes applying regardless of race. However, Northern Rhodesia still taxes Africans only, as does Kenya in fact, at the local level, since only African District Councils impose the tax. Nyasaland applies a higher rate to Europeans, and Southern Rhodesia does so, in effect, by placing all persons in various African areas in the £2 rate class instead of the £12 class. But any Europeans living in these

[11] Unpublished material prepared by Uganda Ministry of Local Governments, *African Authorities Financial Situation* (Entebbe: 1951).
[12] A wife's income must be included with that of her husband.

70

areas would also have the advantage of the lower rates; Africans living in European areas would pay the high rate if their incomes are sufficient—as many of them are.

There is one final distinction in regard to coverage. The local personal taxes in Sierra Leone, Tanganyika, and Kenya apply only in the rural areas, persons in urban areas paying other taxes, primarily property rates. In Northern Rhodesia, municipalities cannot levy personal taxes, but urban Africans are assessed tax for their home Native Authorities. In other jurisdictions, the tax applies in both rural and urban areas.

PAYE Systems

One of the interesting features of these personal taxes is the use in several jurisdictions of PAYE in collection from employees. In Eastern and Western Nigeria, in which the personal tax is a segment in the income tax structure, PAYE applies in the same fashion as for higher incomes, and tax is thus withheld on a current basis. In Lagos, the employer is required to withhold the income rate in November of each year. Tanganyika requires (since 1961) withholding by employers with ten or more employees of the tax due on the previous year's income. The amounts are withheld in one to three installments in March, April, or May. The employer is notified of the amount to collect for each employee after the filing of information returns.

Southern Rhodesia, also beginning in 1961, requires withholding by all employers, regardless of the number of employees that they have. Employers with fewer than 12 employees account for tax by means of the application of stamps (purchased from revenue offices or post offices and affixed to cards kept for each employee). No returns are required of these employers; control is maintained by periodic check by inspectors on a door-to-door basis. Most households in the larger cities are subject to the requirement so far as their domestic help is concerned. With employers hiring more than 12 persons and some others, the usual return system is employed. A register of these employers is maintained in the district revenue offices, and return forms are supplied. This is one of the few PAYE systems in the world that applies to all employees, including households hiring domestic servants.

PROCEDURE

The general system of operation of the personal taxes differs markedly from that of income taxation. While there are individual differences, all are characterized by a very high degree of local participation in assessment, even with those taxes which are imposed

71

by the central governments. The administration of the flat-rate taxes is simpler than that of the graduated ones, but there are several common aspects.

Rate Determination

With all of the central government[13] personal taxes, the rates are set by the central government legislative body, all being uniform throughout the taxing jurisdiction except in Northern Rhodesia, where higher rates are set for the wealthier jurisdictions than for the poorer ones. Local personal tax rates are set by the local units in all instances: the Tribal Authorities in Sierra Leone (subject, until 1961, to a government-imposed maximum of 25s.), the Local Councils in Ghana, the Native Authorities in Northern Nigeria, the Local Authorities in Western Nigeria, the District Councils (the Lukiko in Buganda) in Uganda, the African District Councils in Kenya, the District Councils in Tanganyika, and the Native Authorities in Nyasaland and Northern Rhodesia. In all instances, however, the central governments exercise some influence by their power to review the budget estimates, and they have direct power to approve the personal tax rates in Sierra Leone and Western Nigeria.

The same jurisdiction responsible for the setting of rates is also responsible for administration and collection, with a few exceptions. In Western Nigeria the local authorities are responsible for assessment (although the assessment committees are appointed by the Western Nigeria government) and collection of the tax which is imposed by the regional government. The Kenya government collects both its own and local personal taxes, with most of the responsibility on the District Commissioner. In Nyasaland, on the other hand, the central government tax is collected through the District Councils.

In Uganda the District Governments have responsibility for administration, but primarily through the county and subcounty offices; the Uganda government has no jurisdiction at all except to encourage better procedures.

Tax Rolls

The extent to which systematic rolls or registers of taxpayers are kept varies among the countries and between urban and rural areas. Uganda has perhaps the most complete register system, particularly in Buganda, lists of taxpayers being kept in registers at the village (*muluka*) and subcounty (*gombolola*) levels, and the lists typed and posted. The same is applicable in Northern Nigeria, where lists

[13] The term "central government" is used, in this context, in the federal systems, to refer to the territorial rather than the federal governments.

are prepared at the village level and passed on via the Native Authorities to the Northern Nigeria Ministry of Local Government. In Eastern Nigeria, lists are prepared at the village level and kept in the division offices of the revenue department. In Kenya, lists are kept in various forms in the district offices, and a central registry of the non-African taxpayers maintained in Nairobi. A wide variety of checks is made to ensure that the registry is complete. Tanganyika with its £100 exemption, and thus a much smaller portion of the population covered, maintains lists in the district offices and, in the cities, in the revenue offices.

In Western Nigeria, Ghana, Northern Rhodesia, and Nyasaland, rolls are maintained to some extent, but apparently much less systematically than in the others. Maintenance of the registers is strictly a function of the local authorities in Western Nigeria and Ghana, of the District Commissioner and his assistants in Northern Rhodesia, and of District Headquarters in Nyasaland, plus a register kept by the village headman.

On the other hand, Lagos and Southern Rhodesia operate their taxes without any form of roll for the usual taxpayer. In the former, widespread publicity is given, and the taxpayer is expected to come to the office and pay. In Southern Rhodesia, with its complete PAYE system, the tax is collected largely through the employers, and house-to-house check is made by inspectors to see that the tax is being paid. In the African areas, a tax register serves as the basis of collection.

Returns

A characteristic difference between personal and income taxes is the absence of any formal system of returns. Typically, for Africans particularly, no returns are used at all, the assessments being made on a register and the tax being collected directly. In Tanganyika, notices of assessment, based either on the previous year's tax or the maximum amount, are sent to non-Africans and a number of higher-income Africans. In Dar es Salaam, for example, returns are sent to 6,000 Africans and 22,000 non-Africans. If the recipients of the assessment notices seek a reduction in tax below the stated figure, they must file a simple return showing their income and property. If the request is granted, a new assessment is made. In Kenya, no assessment notices or returns are mailed. Publicity is given to the responsibility for paying tax, and those persons seeking a reduction in tax below the maximum must file a declaration of earnings. These returns are reviewed to see if a reduction is justified. The review is relatively simple, since the revenue departments do not have inspectors and investigators comparable to those of the income tax departments. In Southern Rhodesia likewise, a return is filed only by those nonemployees seeking a reduction of tax below the £12 maximum.

Lagos and Northern Nigeria do not use return forms for the operation of their income rates and community tax, respectively, and Eastern and Western Nigeria do not do so for the personal tax portions of their income taxes (incomes under £100 in Eastern Nigeria). In Uganda a return is prepared, usually by the assessing officials, for each taxpayer.

Responsibility for Assessment

A characteristic feature of the graduated taxes is the ascertainment of the tax liability of most persons by a local assessment committee rather than on the basis of returns examined in a central office. Uganda presents the most sophisticated version of this approach. In Buganda, Teso, and other districts, basic responsibility for assessment rests at the village level. The assessment committee, unlike that in other parts of Africa, is made up primarily of officials. The assessment committees in Buganda consist of the subcounty (*gombolola*) chief, two village (*muluka*) chiefs, two persons selected by *muluka* council, two selected from the *gombolola* council from outside the *muluka*, and two elder citizens chosen by the *muluka* council. The committee typically visits each home or place of business and lists the assessment on the prescribed form; the *gombolola* chief, who often does not accompany the committee, may alter an assessment, but rarely does. Appeal may be made to the county (*ssaza*) chief, whose decision is final.

In Western Nigeria, the local assessment committee is appointed by the Ministry of Local Government but operates autonomously; in Eastern Nigeria, the committee functions under the supervision of the division revenue officer. Personnel consists of respected elders of the village or city. In Kenya, each District Commissioner works out his own system, but in all instances (except in the cities), he is aided by local assessment committees made up of chiefs and elders of each locality in making the actual assessments. The revenue department assessors make the assessments in the cities. There is substantial variation in practice among districts. In Northern Nigeria, the village headman is responsible for assessment of individuals, and while there are no formal assessment committees in the Uganda-Kenya sense, he is typically advised by elders.

The Tanganyika system is slightly different. As in Kenya, in the cities the revenue officer makes the assessments. In the rural areas, responsibility rests on the District Commissioner; in practice his staff of tax clerks, selected mainly on the basis of their prestige in the district, does the actual assessing, in cooperation with the chief of the village. There is no formal assessment committee. Thus more responsibility is placed on the district office, and less on village committees. In Southern Rhodesia, likewise, there is greater centralization. In the African areas the Native Commissioner makes the listings on the basis of the tax register upon consultation with the headmen of the village.

Lagos is the major exception to the committee rule (although of course it has no rural areas); there are no assessment committees, assessment being made by the Federal income tax department, which administers the income rate in the city as well as the income tax.

Methods of Assessment

The most scientific assessment is that in Uganda,[14] and particularly in Buganda. Ten income classes of taxpayers are established. Taxpayers are placed in particular classes according to an estimate of total income received, which, in turn, is based, for the typical Buganda farmer, upon the number of coffee trees and cattle that he has, the area in cotton, and the like, plus income received from labor and other sources. The return form lists the various items to be considered. So far as farming is concerned, assessment is based upon what may be regarded as a typical output of the particular item—i.e., of a coffee tree—rather than the actual figure for the particular year (subject to modifications made when adverse weather conditions, for example, destroy the crop). Thus in large measure the assessed income reflects what the person should be earning, given his acreage, cattle, trees, etc., rather than what he actually earns—the type of tax on income which should increase rather than impair incentives toward maximum efficiency in production.

A defense for the equity of this approach is to be found in the following statement by the government of Buganda:

No African would understand why another African who owned several hundred acres of coffee and mismanaged the estate in such a way that he could prove he had made no income out of it would be able to escape entirely from paying tax, when a small man who breeds ducks for sale on an acre plot and who made a profit, is taxed on this income. . . .[15]

Except on plantations, which are rare in Uganda, no attempt is made to deduct expenses of production, in part because most of the labor, the chief cost element, is supplied by members of the family. For nonfarming activities, income is assessed according to actual

[14] For a general review, see *Memorandum for the Guidance of African Authorities in the Development of Their Direct Personal Taxation Systems* (Entebbe: Ministry of Local Government, 1960); A. C. Badenoch, "Graduated Taxation in the Teso District of Uganda," *Journal of Local Overseas Administration*, Vol. I (January, 1962), pp. 15–22.

[15] *Memorandum Prepared by the Treasury of H.H. The Kabaka's Government of Buganda for the Fiscal Commission* (Kampala: 1962), pp. 19–20.

75

wages and salaries earned. For retailers, if actual figures are not available, it is assumed, in Teso, for example, that 5% of turnover consists of net profit. In practice, in some of the Uganda districts, there is a tendency to assess certain types of occupations, such as cattle dealers, at a flat rate because of the difficulties of ascertaining income, a practice which tends to lessen the equity of the tax. Also, in some areas there is still a tendency to use particular forms of wealth as evidences of income, but the Uganda government has been urging the districts to move away from this, and the wealth basis leads to many taxpayer protests.

In the other countries, so far as the rural areas are concerned, there is little scientific assessment to ascertain income as such. Instead, the assessment committees or officers will grade persons according to their knowledge of the general financial position of the taxpayers, with substantial use of external criteria, such as the size of the house, ownership of cattle, bicycle, motor vehicle, or other items. In other words, tax liability is not actually measured by income, but by very rough indices, in terms of wealth or consumption thereof. This is particularly true in the three regions of Nigeria and in rural Kenya and Tanganyika. In Northern Nigeria, for farmers there is substantial reliance on figures of typical potential earnings for particular acreages and crops, as in Uganda, but in less scientific fashion. In the cities of Northern Nigeria, set rates are often used for particular occupations regardless of actual earnings; the figures vary widely among districts and have not been raised as incomes have increased. Under present policy, the Northern Nigeria government is seeking to ensure that these groups are assessed on the basis of actual income and taxed at standard rates in all Native Authorities.

In the urban areas in Southern Rhodesia, Kenya, and Tanganyika, the assessment is more closely related to income, particularly with employees and larger traders. All three of these governments assess non-Africans and higher-income Africans at the maximum tax unless they file returns to prove that a lower tax is warranted.

Exemptions

Certain exemptions are written into the Acts, such as of persons under eighteen (twenty-one in Sierra Leone), full-time students, and the like. In addition, the power is given to exempt completely persons who are ill, destitute, or otherwise unable to pay. This power is, in fact, usually exercised by the person directly responsible for the operation of the tax in the area. These are the District Commissioners in rural Tanganyika, Kenya, and Nyasaland, and the Revenue Officers in the urban areas of the first two countries named plus urban Southern Rhodesia; the Native Commissioners in African areas of Southern Rhodesia; the Assessment Committees typically in other areas. Lagos is one of the few jurisdictions to provide no exemption of this type at all, although a person earning no income is not required to pay tax.

Thus this basic exemption of the destitute is exercised by administrative discretion, a rule rarely found in income tax legislation. Usually, however, the power is used moderately; the number of otherwise eligible taxpayers exempted on this basis would rarely exceed 5% of the total number of taxpayers. In some jurisdictions permanent exemption is provided for the disabled, old persons, etc.; in others, the exemptions are made on an annual basis only.

Collection

Direct responsibility for collection in the rural areas is placed upon the District Commissioners or their equivalent in Tanganyika, Southern Rhodesia, Northern Rhodesia, and Kenya. In Kenya, both personal and African District Council taxes are administered in this way, actual collection usually being handled by the chiefs. In Nyasaland, the District Council is responsible for collection, and the local treasurer is paid a fee for collection. In Northern Nigeria, the Native Authorities are responsible for collection, the actual work being done usually by the village head or scribe. In the urban areas of East and Central Africa, the revenue offices are responsible for collection, and in Kenya the central office in Nairobi collects for all non-Africans. The Federal revenue offices collect in Lagos.

In Uganda and West Africa, typically the collection is much more decentralized. In Uganda, the subcounty (in Buganda the *gombolola*) chief is the collector; he transmits the funds to the county (*ssaza*) chief, who exercises supervision over the general process of collection. In Ghana, each local council hires its collector on a salary or fee basis. In Western Nigeria, the collector is appointed by the chief or local council, upon which responsibility for collection rests. In Eastern Nigeria, some 13,000 collectors, working on a fee basis of 6% of the amount collected, are locally appointed; they also typically serve as tax agents for the local councils on a fee basis to collect the local poll tax. In Sierra Leone, the village headmen are responsible for collection; this system was partially responsible for the tax riots of 1955, because the headmen were often collecting more than the tax due, sometimes several times as much.

The receipts issued by the collectors, taking the form of tax tickets in Eastern Nigeria and some other areas, are of key importance for enforcement, as noted below. In the urban areas standard receipt books or forms are employed.

Enforcement

Varying methods are used to force payment. In most rural areas there appear to be few troubles; collection is made on the spot, and seldom is there outright refusal to pay. In the areas in which the District Commissioner is responsible for collection he may visit the villages and check the census or other rolls to see that payments have been made. This is common in Kenya and Nyasaland. In Southern Rhodesia a house-to-house check is made by the inspectors, to ensure that the householders have themselves paid and have deducted tax on their employees, household or otherwise. A more common practice, mainly to catch migrant workers and others with no established home, is to establish roadblocks and check all persons passing; if they do not have their tax receipts, they must pay on the spot. This method is used in Northern Rhodesia, Kenya, Ghana, Eastern and Western Nigeria, and Uganda, in all cases with a certain amount of protest. In Tanganyika in the past, inspectors could stop persons and demand tax receipts, taking the person to the local tax office if he could not produce one. At the moment, this procedure does not appear to be regarded as politically feasible.

The problem of collection in the urban areas from the lower income groups is much more difficult. There is a constant shifting of population, particularly in the crowded West African cities, and it is very hard to catch all residents of a house, particularly if the inspector calls in the daytime. Lagos finds a check of the market sellers to be more effective than house-to-house or street checks.

Failure to pay on time results in a penalty—often 50%, but double the tax in Southern Rhodesia. Ultimately, continued failure to pay, particularly in urban areas, brings court action. In Eastern Nigeria, property can be attached and sold without court action, but this procedure is rarely followed. In urban areas in Tanganyika, a summons is obtained from the magistrate, and the delinquent can be jailed, but this practice is uncommon. Court action is brought in urban areas of Kenya after demand notices are sent, and in Uganda, the action takes the form of a civil suit. In the past, in Uganda, occasionally delinquents were jailed for a few days.

Various other enforcement devices are employed. A very significant one, in view of the importance attached to voting in Africa today, is the requirement in Uganda and Nyasaland that tax must be paid before a person can vote. Tanganyika and other jurisdictions ensure that tax is paid before trade, automobile, and other licenses will be issued, and Tanganyika requires evidence of payment of tax before a passport will be issued. Southern Rhodesia uses a unique method of checking that tax is being withheld on employees under the stamp system; the revenue offices keep a close watch on tax stamp sales in various areas. When sales lag, inspectors are sent into the area.

Effectiveness of Operation

Any scientific appraisal of these taxes is very difficult, and the following observations are based in large measure on the comments of persons long familiar with the operation of the taxes in the various countries. It should be noted initially that the taxes are very broad in their application; for example, in Tanganyika, prior to the establishment of the £100 exemption, there were 1.7 million taxpayers out of a population of 9.2 million, with women at that time exempted. Nyasaland has some 600,000 taxpayers out of a population of 2.5 million (women are not taxable); and Kenya had 846,806 in 1961 out of a population of 6 million. In Buganda, there are about 450,000 taxpayers out of an adult male population of perhaps 500,000; in Lagos City (with women taxable), there are an estimated 125,000 out of a population of 350,000.

In several countries, the rolls are believed to be almost entirely complete in rural areas, as, for example, Tanganyika, Northern Rhodesia, Northern Nigeria, and Kenya (urban and rural). In some, like Tanganyika, doubt is expressed about the completeness in urban areas with their shifting populations. In Uganda, the rolls are relatively complete except for some workers with no established homes. On the other hand, rolls are believed to be relatively incomplete in Sierra Leone (where census figures are far out of line with taxpayer totals) and in Western Nigeria. In the latter jurisdiction, it was estimated in 1957 that 26% of the potential taxpayers evaded payment completely. In Ibadan it was estimated that half of the potential taxpayers escaped. Delinquency also varies; it is of minor consequence in Northern Nigeria, for example, with strong Native Authority government and its long tradition of direct tax-paying. Any authority showing more than 5% delinquency is subject to action by the Northern Nigeria government which reduces its autonomy. On the other hand, even in Uganda, it is estimated that in some districts 20% of the persons who should be subject are not paying. In one county, for 1961, 3,000 taxpayers out of 73,000 had failed to pay.

Perhaps the most unsatisfactory situation is to be found in Ghana, in which an estimated 25% to 40%[16] of the persons subject to the personal tax have not been paying it. Administration of the tax in Ghana is entirely in local hands, and effective collection has not been attained. There are several reasons: the long-standing hostility toward the payment of direct tax and its association with colonial-

[16] See *Report of the Commissioner for Local Government Enquiries* (Accra, 1960).

ism, and the substantial amount of migratory labor. One peculiarity of the Ghana tax interferes with effective collection. Payment of tax in one jurisdiction frees the person from liability in another; thus there is a tendency to pay in a low-tax jurisdiction. The range in rates is very wide.

Much more doubt can be raised about the quality of assessment so far as the graduated taxes are concerned. Without question, only a very rough sort of equity is attained; as noted, usually no very careful attempt is made to ascertain income. Yet the results, particularly with relatively careful administration in such countries as Uganda, are probably as satisfactory as can be attained under the conditions prevailing. Clearly, the results are better in the countries with a reasonably scientific approach, such as Uganda, than they are in areas such as Northern Nigeria, which has excellent collection standards but seriously limited assessment procedures. The same is largely true in Western Nigeria, where, as in Eastern Nigeria, charges of political interference with local assessment are sometimes heard. Even in Uganda, there are rumors that assessments will sometimes be adjusted for political reasons.

Taxpayers by Income Class

In only a few countries are results tabulated by income class. (See Table 5.6.)

These figures show the great concentration, so far as Africans are concerned, in the lowest income brackets, but a substantial classification in other brackets. It is obvious that in Buganda too few persons are classified in the top brackets.

In Northern Nigeria there are only 58,000 taxpayers on the "wealthy" lists of the Native Authorities indicating above-average income.

CONCLUSION

Perhaps more than any other feature of African taxation, the personal taxes, particularly those which are graduated, reflect an adaptation of tax structure to the conditions of the countries. Directly and immediately they arose (except in Northern Nigeria, where they were indigenous) out of the desire of the British colonial administration to obtain some revenue from all persons, to lessen reliance on customs duties, and to encourage persons to enter the commercial sector of the economy by selling produce or working for a wage. In their crude form of uniform poll tax their revenue potentialities were limited, since the rate could not exceed the figure tolerable for the lowest-income taxpayers, and they violated not only the usually accepted principles of taxation but also the basic

TABLE 5.6 TAX CLASS OF TAXPAYERS IN SELECTED AREAS

Buganda–1960		Teso (Uganda)	
Tax Rate (shillings)	Number of Taxpayers	Tax Rate (shillings)	Number of Taxpayers
10 (reduced)	6,616	21 (reduced)	2,639
30 (basic)	307,514	40 (basic)	48,903
40	95,808	55	45,032
60	23,559	70	7,640
80	8,470	85	1,052
120	7,227	100	871
200	803	125	809
300	43	150	529
400	29	200	224
		300	39
		400	32
			107,770
		Exempt: partial	2,639
		total	258

SOURCES: Uganda Ministry of Finance; *Journal of Local Overseas Administration, op. cit.*

Kenya—1961				
Income Group (pounds)	Europeans	Asians	Arabs and Somalis	Africans
Under 120	312	3,831	18,696	791,664
120–160	576	1,692	1,552	30,953
161–200	126	1,156	586	10,572
Over 200	24,231	40,542	1,123	13,617
Total Taxpayers	25,245	47,221	21,957	846,806

SOURCE: Data compiled by Government of Kenya.

concepts of equity of the people of the countries. Thus the graduated tax has evolved, bringing both greater revenue possibilities and greater accord with equity. By avoiding the complications of the usual income tax, particularly of the British variety, administration on a reasonably satisfactory basis is possible for the income groups for which it is designed. With no allowances or other refinements it is clearly unsuited as a sole direct tax on the higher income groups —but in all these countries these groups are reached by an income tax of the usual form.

By the reliance on local assessment committees whose members are familiar with the general income status of families, a greater equity in assessment is likely to be attainable than by any other system under the circumstances, despite some inevitable intrusion at times of political influence or personal favoritism. Actually, such charges are much less widespread than might be anticipated. Clearly, the tax has reached the highest state of development in Uganda; it would appear that Ghana, a leader in many other aspects of African economic and governmental development, has lagged behind the others in improving the operation of the tax. As in other aspects of taxation, the levy functions most successfully in countries with a long-standing respect for government, and a minimum of hostility toward government as an instrument of colonialism—Uganda and Northern Nigeria being the prime examples.

SELECTED REFERENCES

Hicks, U. K., *Development from Below*. Oxford: Oxford University Press, 1961.

Orewa, G. Oka, *Taxation in Western Nigeria*. Oxford: Oxford University Press for the Nigerian Institute of Social and Economic Research, 1962.

"Methods of Direct Taxation in British Tropical Africa." *Journal of African Administration*, Vol. 2 and Vol. 3 (October, 1950; January, 1951; and October, 1951), pp. 3–12, 30–41, and 77–87.

Cox-George, N. A., *Finance and Development in West Africa: The Sierra Leone Experiment*. London: Dobson, 1961.

Report of the Uganda Fiscal Commission. Entebbe: Government Printer, 1962.

Government of Kenya, *Report of the Fiscal Commission*. Nairobi: Government Printer, 1963.

6 Customs, Excise, and Export Duties[1]

T RADITIONALLY, customs duties have constituted the major source of revenue in countries in early stages of economic and political development. Instituted for revenue purposes only, they have typically constituted the sole significant revenue source which was feasible for administration under such conditions. As the economies have expanded, the customs have tended to decline in importance. As the foreign trade sector becomes a relatively smaller element in the economy as a whole, other taxes have developed, and the inequities of the customs system have become more widely recognized. In turn, the customs systems have tended to shift in emphasis from revenue to protection.

REVENUE IMPORTANCE

Customs alone yield 61% of the revenues of Sierra Leone, the least developed of the countries. In Sierra Leone, Ghana, Nigeria, and Tanganyika, customs and excises combined yield over 60% of total tax revenues. On the other hand, they yield only 28.3% in the Federation of Rhodesia and Nyasaland. Direct taxes yield only 9% in Zanzibar and 15% in Ghana. The export duties, which

[1] Portions of this chapter appeared in the January–February, 1963, issue of the *Canadian Tax Journal* and are used by permission of the Canadian Tax Foundation.

Rhodesia and Kenya do not use, and of which Tanganyika makes only nominal use, provide 45% of Zanzibar's revenue (mostly from cloves) and nearly 20% of Ghana's (primarily from cocoa), as shown in Table 6.1.

TABLE 6.1   CUSTOMS, EXCISES, EXPORT DUTIES, AND OTHER
TAXES AS PERCENTAGES OF TOTAL
TAX REVENUES
1961–1962 BUDGET ESTIMATES

Country	Customs Duties	Excises	Total, Customs and Excises	Export Duties	Other Indirect Taxes	Direct Taxes*
Sierra Leone§	60.7	neg.†	60.7	7.2	2.2	29.9
Ghana	55.4	6.2	61.6	19.2	4.7	14.5
Nigeria‡	57.6	6.4	64.0	14.1	0.9	21.0
Kenya	34.3	12.1	46.4	0	9.5	44.1
Uganda	38.8	16.9	55.7	14.9	5.5	23.9
Tanganyika	49.0	14.8	63.8	0.2	5.7	30.3
Zanzibar	44.5	0	44.5	45.4	0.7	9.4
Rhodesia‡	22.6	5.7	28.3	0	4.3	67.4

* Income, company, and personal taxes.
† More significant in subsequent years.
‡ Federal government and territories combined.
§ 1960–1961.

THE TARIFF STRUCTURES

An understanding of the customs systems requires consideration of the tariff structures and of the operating procedures. This section is concerned with the first question, the next with that of procedures. As previously noted, Kenya, Uganda, and Tanganyika have a common tariff system and will be treated as a unit in the following discussion.

General Tariff Policy

There is substantial variation in emphasis among the six jurisdictions so far as the general purpose of the tariffs is concerned. Two, Sierra Leone and Zanzibar, which are the least developed industrially, still adhere to the traditional policy of levying customs duties for revenue purposes only. In the other four, revenue plays an important—if not the major—role, but other considerations play a part as well. Protection has played the most significant role in Rhodesia, and lesser roles in East Africa, Nigeria, and Ghana.

Rhodesia has, relatively, much more industry than the other areas. While some of these industries, such as tobacco, building materials, smelting, and food processing, have developed without the need for protection, other industries, particularly clothing, furniture, and tires, have been given substantial tariff protection. With a relatively small market (Rhodesia has about 8 million people, but the great majority are barely above subsistence living), a strong bias for imported goods, and the well-established industry of South Africa close at hand, protection has been regarded as imperative for most new industries to develop.

In East Africa, most of the demand for protection has come from Kenya, which has enjoyed the most rapid industrialization, partly because of a larger European population, partly because of its location in the center of British East Africa. This demand has caused considerable complaint from Uganda and Tanganyika, which have maintained that they are forced to pay more for their goods while Kenya gains from the industry. But in recent years industrialization has increased in the other two countries as well. Though for the most part the three countries reconcile their differences and agree on a common tariff, there are a few instances in which they have not, and the tariffs differ. The major items of difference are petroleum products, aluminum sheeting, and certain farm products. The major areas in which protection has been important are clothing, processed foods, and coffee.

In the remaining two countries, the protection element has been present to only a minor extent, while other aspects, in addition to revenue, have been much more significant in shaping policy. Nigeria and Ghana have raised tariffs for protective reasons in a few instances, but actually this has been a minor consideration in tariff policy. Both are giving more attention to the question as industrial development continues. On the other hand, beginning in 1961, Ghana has stressed tariff increases as a means of lessening balance-of-payments difficulties, of curtailing over-all consumer spending, and of freeing foreign exchange for items of major importance for economic growth. Sharp increases were made for this purpose on many luxury items in 1961, and a so-called purchase tax (described in the last section of this chapter) was added. The changes were made primarily on the basis of the recommendations of the British economist Kaldor, who, as an adviser to the government, recommended a strong "austerity" program to check foreign exchange deficits and encourage savings. Nigeria has thus far not introduced similar austerity programs, but in recent budget messages considerable attention has been given to the need for curtailment of consumption of imported luxury items, particularly those for which home-produced substitutes are available.

Concessions to Industry

In all of the jurisdictions except Zanzibar, provision is made for the granting of concessions on duty for various industries. These take the form of suspension, rebate, or refund of duty on specified materials, supplies, and equipment for new industry (and in some instances for established ones as well), either for a temporary period or indefinitely. As subsequently noted, much of this equipment is entirely free of duty. The concessions are relevant in those instances in which duty would otherwise apply. In Ghana and Sierra Leone the concessions are made for the first several years (Sierra Leone, typically five) of the operation of new firms upon specific application and approval by the Minister. The power has thus far been used only in three or four instances in Sierra Leone, and sparingly in Ghana. Nigeria provides the concession through a refund system, with control largely in the hands of the Minister of Trade and Commerce. The regions, which share in customs revenue, are compensated by the Federal government for these amounts.

In East Africa and Rhodesia the adjustments (called rebates in the latter) are made upon an industry-wide basis, rather than by application and approval for particular firms only. In East Africa, proposals are reviewed by a Tariff Committee, made up of representatives of the three governments. In Rhodesia, decisions are made by the Minister of Finance or by legislative action. Neither East Africa nor Rhodesia has pioneer companies legislation providing general tax relief for new industries, as is found in West Africa.

The Rate Structures

Two of the tariff structures have preferential features. Sierra Leone uses a two-column tariff, with preference for the United Kingdom and Commonwealth countries. The Rhodesia tariff is a four-column tariff, with the lowest rate for the United Kingdom and its colonies, and successively higher ones for self-governing dominions of the Commonwealth, most-favored-nation countries, and others—a small group with which there is little trade. The tariffs also differ widely in the degree of detail; those for which protection is nonexistent or a minor element, including the West African countries and Zanzibar, are relatively simple, with listing by major categories. The East African tariff, with 177 items, is more detailed, especially in the categories for which protection is desired. The most complicated is the Rhodesia tariff, with 331 items and many subcategories. Even so, the tariff is regarded as unsatisfactory because the nomenclature and breakdowns are somewhat obsolete and no longer entirely suited to the industrial economy which has developed.

All of the jurisdictions make some use of both specific and ad valorem rates. The three West African countries emphasize the latter, except for the ones on which specific rates are traditional—liquor, motor fuel, other petroleum products, and tobacco products. But these countries to some extent, and East Africa and Rhodesia to a much greater extent, employ a dual system on certain classes of commodities. Both specific and ad valorem rates are provided, the actual duty being the higher of the two. With this structure the ad valorem rate is usually the higher on typical importations, while the specific alternative is designed to ensure a reasonable minimum on very cheap goods and where dumping or undiscovered undervaluation occurs. Piece goods are almost always given dual rates; other examples from the East African tariff include onions, condensed milk, clothing, footwear, fabrics, bicycles, enamelware, metal sheets, soap, ink, and phonograph records. In East Africa, 55% of the revenue comes from ad valorem duties, 45% from specific duties. Several of the major imported goods, of course, are those subject to traditional specific duties. The specific rates are simpler but discriminate against cheaper articles and are unsuited for some types of commodities.

In the rate structures themselves, several principles play a part, along with a considerable element of chance and influence of tradition.

1. "Luxury" considerations. In all of the tariffs, the attempt is made to place relatively high rates—in fact, the highest—on items regarded as unessential for the basic family budget. In large measure in the past, and still today in considerable degree, the bulk of the burden on luxury goods is borne by non-Africans.

Categories singled out in this fashion include:

    a. Liquor. Whiskey and other distilled spirits typically bear the highest of all duties. Since the duties are specific, they cannot be compared easily with the prices, but not uncommonly they reach 100% of price, exclusive of duty. For example, the East African rate is 160s. per proof gallon; in Nigeria 140s., Rhodesia 82½s., Zanzibar 100s.

    b. Cigarettes and other tobacco products.

    c. Consumer durables and miscellaneous luxury goods. For example, note the following typical items:

	Sierra Leone*	Ghana	Nigeria	East Africa	Zanzibar	Rhodesia*
Bicycles	5	5	20	25	$22\frac{1}{2}$	15
Motor Vehicles	$7\frac{1}{2}$	15	20	15	15	$20-37\frac{1}{2}$
Radios	10	45	20	25	$22\frac{1}{2}$	25
Musical Instruments	30	30	20	25	$22\frac{1}{2}$	20
Cameras	—	—	$33\frac{1}{3}$	ex.	ex.	20
Jewelry	—	50	$33\frac{1}{3}$	$33\frac{1}{3}$	$22\frac{1}{2}$	35
Perfume	50	100	75	$66\frac{2}{3}$	45	30
Cosmetics	15	75	$66\frac{2}{3}$	45	40	30

* Commonwealth preference rate.
— Not available.

> d. Luxury processed foods. Candy, for example, bears rates of 30% in Sierra Leone, 50% in Ghana and Nigeria, 25% in East Africa, 20% in Zanzibar, 15% in Rhodesia (Commonwealth). Canned meat and canned fruit typically have rates of 20% or more.

2. Widespread use. Most countries, while exempting certain basic necessities, apply duties to some goods of widespread usage such as wearing apparel and piece goods, primarily as a revenue source. In some instances, protective elements are involved; the goods of widespread use are frequently ones for which domestic production is most feasible.

3. Necessities. Very low rates or complete exemption is given to goods which are regarded either as basic necessities, as important to the general welfare, such as educational materials, or are used primarily in agriculture and industry. These categories include:

> a. Basic foodstuffs, particularly unprocessed ones. Examples include fresh fruit and vegetables, fresh meat, eggs, butter, fish.
>
> b. Medicines and drugs, almost universally exempt.
>
> c. Books and most other printed matter.
>
> d. Seeds.
>
> e. Industrial and farm machinery.
>
> f. Basic building materials (except where protection for home industry is desired).
>
> g. Pig iron, steel, and other metals in nonfabricated form, typically exempt, or subject to rates of 10% or less.

In addition, rebates or refunds of duty on materials, supplies, and equipment used in various approved industry rates are provided, as noted above.

4. Protective elements. These are not usually obvious from looking at the rate tables, but appear from an examination of actual policy on various goods. Major instances were noted above. The elements are most common with clothing, processed food, and cigarettes.

Most of the countries use a substantial number of ad valorem rates, despite attempts to group commodities into a small number of rate classes. For example, the basic East African schedule is as follows: general revenue, 25%; reduced rate for seminecessities, and for limited protection, $12\frac{1}{2}$%; primary protection, $33\frac{1}{3}$%; luxury, $66\frac{2}{3}$%. But this schedule is by no means followed entirely.

Table 6.2 shows typical items in the major ad valorem rate classes in East Africa; there are a few items with 40% and 15% rates. It should be noted that the food items with relatively high rates are ones being protected.

In Rhodesia, the luxury rates are lower than is typical elsewhere, frequently 40–30–30–20, with protective rates of 30–20–20–10, and lower rates on seminecessities of 20–10–free–free. There is a tendency to place some duty (except on imports from Commonwealth countries) on many goods that are completely exempt in other countries.

The Catchall Category

A major problem in tariff construction is the treatment of the "not otherwise specified" category—of the rate to apply to all items not specifically listed. This is particularly important with the relatively brief tariffs of Ghana and Nigeria, but significant as well with others. Zanzibar with its revenue-only tariff, has no catchall category, and no duty applies on nonspecified items. This approach causes considerable loss of potential revenue, and inequity. The others all have specified rates, as follows:

Sierra Leone	25%, preferential; 37%, regular
Ghana	30%
Nigeria	20%
East Africa	25%
Rhodesia	10%, United Kingdom; 20%, Commonwealth; $22\frac{1}{2}$%, most-favored-nation; 30%, other

These figures are reasonably typical of the rates on luxury goods. Unfortunately, however, they catch many miscellaneous items

TABLE 6.2 ITEMS INCLUDED IN MAJOR AD VALOREM RATE CLASSES IN EAST AFRICA

Exempt	$12\frac{1}{2}\%$	25%	$33\frac{1}{3}\%$	$66\frac{2}{3}\%$
meat	dates	salmon	butter	flavorings
wheat	cocoa	canned	cheese	toilet prep-
flour	dried	fish	macaroni	arations
rice	fruit	onions	tomato	perfume
cassava	hops	milk	purée	
raw coffee	nails	cream	clothing	
fish	bolts	table salt	fabrics	*Relatively*
fresh fruit	windows	footwear	enamelware	*High*
fresh	scales	thread	jewelry	*Specific*
vegetables	putty	bicycles		*Rates*
seeds	plate glass	aluminum		
fish nets	marble	sheets		liquor
farm	plywood	razor		cigarettes
equipment	printing	blades		motor fuel
industrial	paper	asbestos		
equipment	flooring	sheets		
base metals,		soap		
bars, plates		food dyes		
ore		ink		
tractors	*15%*	clocks		
printing		watches		
equipment	motor	phonograph		
railway	vehicles	records		
equipment				
telephone				
equipment				
refrigeration				
equipment				
coal				
chemicals				
drugs and				
medicines				
surgical				
equipment				
books				
school				
equipment				

used primarily in industry or agriculture that are not specified as exempt. In part, this difficulty is overcome by the special refunds or rebates to the industries, but by no means entirely so.

Any exact comparison of over-all duty levels is difficult, but from careful review it would appear that Ghana and Nigeria have the highest over-all levels (except on certain items given strong protection elsewhere), with the lowest rates in Rhodesia (Commonwealth preference rates) and Zanzibar.

CUSTOMS OPERATION

Many aspects of customs operation are standard among virtually all countries, and thus no detailed exposition is required. However, major steps will be outlined.

Procedure

In the West African countries, East Africa, and Zanzibar virtually all imports come by ship. Rhodesia, on the other hand, has no ports and is one of the very few countries in the world where virtually all imports arrive by rail. However, by agreement with the Portuguese, customs officers are maintained at Beira and Lourenço Marques in Portuguese East Africa, and much of the clearing is done at dockside. These two ports account for most of the importations; some occur through South African ports and a limited amount via Angola and the Benguela Railway. The various steps in the operation of the systems are listed briefly below primarily in terms of imports by ship, with some notation of Rhodesian procedure.

1. First, the steamship line must provide a manifest, which lists all cargo to be landed in the port, within 24 hours after landing. The manifest is usually sent ahead by air mail. In Rhodesia, the railway provides a separate slip for each arriving shipment.

2. The importer (or his broker) files a customs bill of entry, listing the commodities, rate classifications, and other data. The invoices are attached.

3. The bills of entry are checked by clerks for completeness, and then sent to the assessing officers, who make a careful check and assess the duty. In smaller ports, one person will do both jobs.

4. Meanwhile, the bills of entry are checked off against the manifest items.

5. The importer is notified of the duty and, upon payment of it, may obtain release of the goods. In Rhodesia, the railway notifies the shipper that the goods are available.

6. The goods meanwhile have been unloaded from the ship or railway car into the warehouse. The officer in charge of the warehouse checks the shipments against the bills of entry, and opens for examination of actual contents any items that he regards as questionable. The percentage of shipments actually checked visibly is from 20% to 25% in East Africa and less than 10% in Rhodesia. Some major types of shipments, of course, such as coal, require no specific check. Bulk shipments may be loaded directly on railway

cars rather than being transferred twice. In Rhodesia, carload shipments to industrial sidings are cleared by advance arrangement to avoid unloading and reloading.

Where mislabeling or false description of weight, etc., is discovered, a penalty is applied, much heavier if fraud is suspected than if the error appears to be an honest one.

Goods in the shipment that are not claimed, or ones on which duty is not paid, are sent to the Queen's warehouse and after two months or more are sold at public auction.

Appraisal

With ad valorem tariffs, the key to correct payment of duty is accurate valuation of the goods subject to duty. The West African countries, East Africa, and Zanzibar all define value in terms of the Brussels Convention, as the open-market sale price from a seller in the home country to a buyer in the importing country, delivered to the port of importation. Thus, primary reliance is placed on actual selling prices. Rhodesia, however, follows the South African–Canadian–United States practice of valuation on the basis of whichever is the highest of (1) the FOB sale price by the exporter to the importer, or (2) the domestic price in the exporting country, that is, the price at which goods are freely offered to all wholesale channels (plus the extra cost of packing and shipping for export). Thus it is necessary for the customs department to review domestic prices of the goods, at least when there is any doubt. This procedure, designed to ensure more adequate duty on goods sold more cheaply abroad than at home, creates various problems. In some instances, for example, the exporting firm may not sell to independent wholesalers but only to his own subsidiaries, and in other instances a wide range of discounts is given. The department seeks, under such circumstances, to arrive at a figure which appears to be reasonable. It is necessary to keep investigators in South Africa and Great Britain, the two major sources of supply, to check upon domestic prices; for other countries, information is obtained by occasional trips of the investigators or by correspondence.

In none of the countries is complete reappraisal made of all goods; Rhodesia is the most careful in the checking of value figures shown on invoices. Sierra Leone has no valuation staff at all; and only limited staffs are employed in Nigeria and Ghana for this purpose. In all three, prime reliance is placed on the apparent reasonableness of the prices as shown on the invoice, with reference by the assessing clerks to higher officials if there is doubt. East Africa does not make a serious reappraisal, depending upon the assessing clerk's reaction to the reasonableness of the figures, and upon a file developed by the Investigation and Valuation Branch of "uplifts" to be applied on transactions between affiliated companies. This branch, which was established in 1959, now has 15 employees. One peculiarity in East Africa is the requirement that the importer file a declaration of value, a step which makes prosecution for deliberate misstatement of value easier.

The Zanzibar procedure is similar to that in East Africa, but with a less thorough check upon value.

In Rhodesia the examining officers, who are relatively high-level personnel, review the reported values carefully; it would appear that they are more expert in the field of values than the officers in the other countries. In addition, a special inspectorate reviews the invoices and other documents after clearance for the correctness of the appraisal, and for information to build up a file of valuation figures to use in transactions between affiliated companies and in other cases of doubt. The files gathered from these investigations are made available to all assessing officers.

Origin of Goods

Preferential tariffs give rise to a special and serious problem not found with others, namely, the need for discovering the country of origin. This feature requires an added check, and one often difficult to make. In some instances simple misstatements of origin occur, while in others there is deliberate fraud. More commonly, however, the problem arises over the partial use of materials and parts from nonpreference countries. In Rhodesia, a basic eligibility figure (25%) is set for the percentage of the total cost which must be represented by labor and materials of the Commonwealth country for the preference to apply. Other figures, ranging from 5% to 50%, are set on certain goods.

Enforcement

Customs enforcement involves several steps, some of which have been noted:

1. Detection of mislabeling and misrepresentation on invoices, use of forged invoices and other documents.

2. Detection of discrepancies between actual physical quantities and those reported on the invoices. These can be discovered only by an adequate physical check of shipments and review of invoices.

3. Ascertainment of understatement of values, as noted.

4. Smuggling—the oldest form of tax evasion known to mankind.

It is very difficult to assess the amount of smuggling actually occurring; it would appear that Sierra Leone and Nigeria have the greatest volume. In the former, there is at present no separate preventive force, and inadequate road patrols. The worst problem is that of smuggling diamonds (subject to export duties) out of the country, and of smuggling cigarettes in, mainly from Liberia, on an organized scale.

In Nigeria the problem has been sufficiently serious that it has attracted major attention in the 1961 budget message and in feature newspaper articles in Lagos during 1962. The worst source, by far, is the Spanish island of Fernando Po, just off the coast, from which cigarettes and liquor are smuggled in large quantities in small boats at night. It is estimated that one sixth of all cigarettes consumed in Nigeria have been smuggled in. Other expensive articles also come in unknown amounts. The government has stepped up the work of the Investigation Branch, and is making serious efforts to stop the practice. Some nongovernmental sources suggest that the only solution is for Nigeria to seize and annex the island!

Ghana, partly because of geography, is less troubled, although considerable quantities of cigarettes and liquor do come in, on an unorganized scale. The frontier guard is maintained by the police, not by customs officials, a practice which may lessen effectiveness.

East Africa has one major source of nuisance: the smuggling from Zanzibar, which lies only a few miles off the coast and has substantially lower customs duties. Efforts have been made previously, and are being made again, to bring Zanzibar into the East African customs union. This is mostly a small-scale operation, mainly in cigarettes and piece goods, and seizures are relatively frequent. Elsewhere in East Africa, there is some smuggling across Lake Victoria and the land borders, but only in small quantities. Zanzibar, itself, reports very little smuggling.

Rhodesia has no seacoast problem, but it does have a small amount of land smuggling, some from Mozambique, but primarily from Katanga, in the Congo. The area on the Katanga border is thickly settled, with substantial movement of people both ways, and detection is difficult.

Personnel

In Ghana, Sierra Leone, Zanzibar, and Rhodesia, customs and excise tax administration is under the jurisdiction of the Comptroller of Customs and Excise; in East Africa, the Commissioner of Customs and Excise, a unit in the East Africa Common Services Organization; and in Nigeria, a Board of Customs and Excise. In all instances excise tax administration is combined with that of customs. This administration is completely separate from the income tax administration.

All of the jurisdictions report serious difficulties in getting adequate numbers of competent personnel. The difficulty lies with salary standards, with the very small number of Africans with adequate training, with the lure of other jobs for those who have adequate training, and with the apparent lack of any future for non-Africans in the positions, so far as West and East Africa are concerned. Ghana, Nigeria, and Sierra Leone, which have virtually no potential employees except Africans but have, relatively, more trained Africans than the other countries, report serious difficulty in getting and keeping a competent staff—given the salaries, the conditions of service, and the lure of other jobs. The East African situation is somewhat different. Of some 1,400 employees, 800, holding most of the positions except the very senior and the lowest-paid jobs, are Asians, primarily Indians and Goans. But these persons are fearful of the future, in light of the demands for Africanization; the future for the Europeans (about 80) is probably little better from a long-range point of view. But there are extremely few Africans with the necessary training, and customs work does not appeal to most of those who are properly trained. For the higher positions, the service seeks university graduates, but the total of these in all East Africa is only a few hundred a year, and more attractive jobs are usually available. Zanzibar is also largely staffed by Indians.

Rhodesia reports very serious problems. For years, much of the recruitment was done in the United Kingdom; because of the political uncertainties of the Federation and other factors, this source has dried up. The country itself has too few university graduates annually to provide sufficient numbers. Thus it has been necessary to hire primarily high school graduates (holders of the Cambridge certificate) and train them within the organization. About one fourth of the staff is African, but they hold the lowest-level jobs.

EXCISES

As domestic production of goods subject to duty has increased within the countries, excises have been introduced on those commodities, such as liquor and tobacco, traditionally subject to such levies in Great Britain. The number of commodities subject to excises, however, is still very small; none of these countries has established a widespread system of excises or resorted to a sales tax. The Ghana purchase tax (described at the end of this chapter) is, apart from motor vehicles, little more than a supplement to the customs duties.

Sierra Leone, which had no excises prior to 1960, now has a levy on cigarettes and will, without doubt, impose levies on liquor and beer as factories now under construction begin to produce. Zanzibar has no excises, since it does not produce items potentially subject to these taxes.

The situation for the other taxing jurisdictions is as follows:

Cigarettes are taxed in all the countries. The Ghana and Nigeria rates are ad valorem, in Ghana 45% and 60% of the manufacturer's selling price for light and heavy cigarettes, respectively; in Nigeria 30%, 48%, and 50% for three weight classes. East Africa and Rhodesia tax on the basis of weight, 11s. per pound in the former (with the same rate on other tobacco products); 4/7 on cigarettes and 2/6 on tobacco in Rhodesia.

The Ghana tax on beer is 8/6 per gallon; the Rhodesia rate is 3s. per gallon; the Nigeria rate is 5/6 per gallon of worts, the East Africa rate 6s. per gallon of worts. Soft drinks are taxed only in Nigeria, with a rate of 1/4 per gallon; with the tremendous increase in the consumption of this product in recent years it represents a major potential source for other countries. Liquor is taxed only in Ghana, East Africa, and Rhodesia.[2] The rate in East Africa is 130s. per proof gallon; the Rhodesian rate varies with the percentage of the spirits imported. The rate on whiskey, for example, ranges from 62/6 to 98/6. Sugar and matches are taxed in East Africa only, at a rate of 12.32 per hundredweight on the former and, on matches, per 7,200: 3s. in Kenya, 6.50 in Tanganyika and Uganda.

Almost universally the excises are lower than the customs duty, as would be expected in terms of protection. For example, the East African duty on distilled spirits is 160s. a proof gallon, the excise 130s. The Rhodesia duty is 82/6, while the excise varies with the relative amount of imported spirits, the rate on a proof gallon with less than 40% of imported spirits being 62/6. The Nigeria rates are difficult to compare because one is ad valorem, the other specific. On cigarettes, as another example, the East African excise rate is 11s. per pound, the duty 36s. The Rhodesian duty is 10s. plus 15% ad valorem, the excise 4/7 per pound.

The experience with the administration of these excises has been very satisfactory, the procedures followed being comparable to those in other countries. None of the countries now uses stamps for enforcement purposes; they were used for a time in both East Africa and Rhodesia (prior to federation), but were eliminated to save the costs of printing and the cost and nuisance of control of and accounting for the stamps. The change was regarded as entirely satisfactory.

The exact basis of application of the tax varies somewhat. In Nigeria and East Africa the tax on beer applies to the output before

[2] Ghana refrained from taxing beer and spirits until 1962 in order to end illicit production of poor-quality products.

bottling, the beer being measured in the vats, while Rhodesia taxes the output when it leaves the brewery in terms of actual rather than presumptive output. Cigarettes are taxed when they leave the stockroom. Liquor is taxed in Rhodesia at the time it leaves the distillery, soft drinks in Nigeria on the output after bottling, sugar in East Africa at the time of delivery from the storeroom. In some instances, such as in the cigarette factories in East Africa and the distillery in Rhodesia, an excise officer is kept in the plant at all times; in other instances frequent checks are made. Tax is paid monthly.

Minor problems are encountered by Nigeria with keeping the smaller bottling plants under proper control, but on the whole that country's taxation of soft drinks has worked well. The view expressed in some other countries that soft drinks cannot be taxed satisfactorily is not borne out by Nigerian experience.

There are a few excises imposed by subordinate units in the federal states. Northern Rhodesia and Nyasaland apply a sales tax to motor fuel instead of subjecting it to customs duty, but the tax is collected from the oil distributors by the Federation government. Eastern Nigeria imposes and collects a tax on the sale of motor fuel, as does Kenya. The Kenya levy has been in operation since 1921; the tax is collected when the fuel leaves the bulk plants in Mombasa. The tax is 45¢ on petrol (gasoline), 35¢ on diesel fuel; by the logic of highway finance, the tax should be heavier on the latter.

The experience of Nigeria with two other excises in recent years illustrates the problems in the extension of excise systems to other products. One was an excise on candy. The result of its use was a sharp drop in sales, and complaints of loss of jobs. Consequently, the government repealed the tax. The second was a levy on soap, which reached only the output of factories, and not that of small-scale household production. The result was a substantial shift in usage to the household-made soap, strong complaints from the larger manufacturers, and consequent replacement of the excise by a special duty on caustic soda, which is a necessary ingredient regardless of the form of manufacture.

EXPORT DUTIES

As noted in Table 6.1, export duties yield a significant portion of the revenues of Zanzibar (45.4%), Ghana, Nigeria, and Uganda, and a somewhat smaller percentage in Sierra Leone. These taxes have been very tempting to governments of countries that export in large quantities through marketing boards, since they are very easy to collect and yield large sums of revenue. While these taxes are imposed on a foreign trade transaction and are of the general nature of indirect levies, they are actually, in a sense, income taxes on the primary producers of the exported products, to the extent to which the exported goods are sold at world prices—as is true with most of the commodities involved. On this basis, they are severely condemned by some persons. There is strong feeling in Rhodesia that they should not be used, and also in Kenya and Tanganyika there is prevailing sentiment against them. The basic criticism is that they reduce the incentives to produce and thus retard economic development. At the same time the yields are highly unstable. If they are applied to a product of which the country produces so much as to dominate the world market (the only major example is that of cloves in Zanzibar), the duty may in part be reflected in higher prices and thus the burden in part shifted to the consumers in other countries (apart from the effects of changes in exchange rates), but at the expense of reduced sales and thus output of the product.

A brief review of the systems in the countries using them follows.

Sierra Leone

The primary export duty is the 5% levy on diamonds; the government is reluctant to raise the figure because of increased danger of smuggling. Some smuggling must occur at present, since this is one of the easiest items in the world to conceal. A 14% ad valorem duty is applied to cocoa, coffee, ginger, and a few other items.

Ghana

The export duty on cocoa, by far the country's major export, has been highly productive of revenue. The duty is a rather complicated one which varies with the cocoa prices. The figure of £100 a ton is subtracted from the FOB price; the government takes as duty one half of the excess up to a price of £260 and the entire excess over this figure. The price in recent years has been around £170. There are three others: on diamonds (9%), kola nuts (6d. per 20 pounds), and timber. The timber duty, which has a complex rate schedule, has been growing in importance in recent years.

Nigeria

The system in Nigeria is much more complicated and will merely be summarized:[3]

1. Bananas: 1/6 per bunch
2. Live animals (not for food): £3

[3] There are certain exceptions and special rates on some of the items.

3. Benniseed: 10%
4. Columbite: £1 per ton
5. Cotton lint and cottonseed: 10%
6. Groundnuts (peanuts): 10%
7. Groundnut cake, meal, and oil: 10%
8. Hides: £22 a ton
9. Palm kernels, cake, meal, and oil: 10%
10. Palm oil: 10%
11. Rubber: crepe, 10%; paste, 5%; raw, 10%
12. Shea nuts: £2 10s. per ton
13. Skins: varying rates depending on their nature
14. Tin: ore, 13/6 per ton; metal, £1 1/9 per ton
15. Wood and timber: 1 to 3d. per cubic foot

Uganda

By far the major export duty is that on cotton; both this duty and the one on coffee have cutoff price figures below which the duty does not apply. Since coffee prices in recent years have tended to be below the figure, the yield of the coffee duty has been small. A duty on hides and skins is of minor importance.

Zanzibar

The export duty on cloves yields nearly half of the island's revenue. The current rate is 65s. per hundredweight, collected from the exporters. The rate is equivalent to about a 25% ad valorem duty on the export price. In addition, there are 15% ad valorem export duties on coconuts, copra, and coconut oil, and of 4s. per ton on mangrove bark, which are of minor consequence.

Tanganyika

The Tanganyika export duties are of negligible importance.

THE GHANA PURCHASE TAX

In 1961, Ghana enacted a so-called purchase tax as a supplement to the customs duties on a group of consumer durables and other items. The items and rates are as shown in Table 6.3.

The taxes on motor vehicles are collected from the dealer and must be paid before the license is issued; the taxable price includes customs duties. The others are paid by the importer in conjunction with payment of customs duties. The tax element must be kept separate from the price.

The purpose of the tax, which was enacted on the recommendations of Kaldor in his capacity as an adviser to the Ghana government, was twofold: to reduce imports and thus lessen balance-of-

TABLE 6.3 PURCHASE TAX RATES IN GHANA, 1962

$66\frac{2}{3}\%$	$33\frac{1}{3}\%$	15%	10% to $66\frac{2}{3}\%$ Depending on Size
furniture	sewing machines	bicycles	motor vehicles
refrigerators	typewriters	tricycles	
air conditioners	radios	motorcycles	
musical instruments	record players		
washing machines	tape recorders		
vacuum cleaners	tires and tubes		
floor polishers	stoves		
floor coverings	fans, irons		
watches, clocks	kettles		
cameras	toasters		
projectors	wearing apparel		
phonograph records			

payments difficulties that had developed, and to reduce consumer luxury spending and thus increase savings. The tax on motor vehicles was designed not only to serve these ends but also to encourage purchase of smaller cars. The policy of levying a separate tax instead of raising customs duties was designed primarily to facilitate keeping the tax separate from the price in order to prevent price increases to the consumer in excess of the amount of the tax.

The tax move was not popular, as might be expected. The items subject to the tax included ones regarded as everyday necessities in other countries and which Ghanaians rising into higher income levels looked forward to acquiring. In light of the importance of the desire to elevate levels of living as an incentive to greater productivity and effort, serious questions may be raised about the desirability of such taxation. These are extremely heavy levies by any usual standards, other than the British purchase tax. Apart from the over-all questions, some effects of the tax are highly objectionable and can be avoided without alteration of the basic structure. Motor trucks are subjected to the same rates as cars, and thus a very heavy burden is placed on large trucks. Yet the country is highly dependent on motor transport, and expansion is important for economic development. The failure to allow drawback on goods reexported (95% drawback is allowed on customs duties) was a serious error and impaired some types of trade in Ghana. However, it appears that the program has had at least some success in accomplishing its goals, and reportedly there has been a definite shift in car purchases to smaller, cheaper ones.

7 Taxation of Real Property[1]

THE ROLE OF THE TAXATION of real property in the tax structures of developing economies has been the subject of substantial discussion in recent years. But the studies of this question have largely ignored the practice in this field in former British Africa;[2] even the World Bank studies of the economies of various African countries have paid little attention to the subject. This chapter will review the present practice in the eight countries included in the study. A surprisingly wide variety of practice is found, despite the common British colonial background, resulting from an adaptation of British practice to varying African conditions. African property taxation, except for the European areas of Kenya, is almost solely urban taxation; nowhere is African-owned farm land subject to significant tax. In the urban sector, a sharp divergence of policy is found between West Africa, in which the taxes are imposed almost solely upon buildings, and East and Central Africa, in which they are either imposed solely upon land, or have dif-

[1] For this part of the study, the author is particularly indebted to the officials of the valuation units of Ghana, the Nigerian Federal government, Nairobi, and Bulawayo (Southern Rhodesia).

Portions of this chapter appeared in the February, 1963, issue of *Land Economics*, and are used by permission of the journal.

[2] There is only incidental reference to the question in the major work in the field, *Taxation of Agricultural Land in Underdeveloped Economies*, by H. P. Wald (Cambridge: Harvard University Press, 1959).

ferential rates favoring buildings over land. Where urban property taxes are used, they typically constitute the chief source of municipal tax revenue. As in British practice, the property taxes are referred to as property *rates*.

WEST AFRICA

There have been several basic problems in developing suitable taxation of real property in West Africa. The West African cities, unlike their East and Central African counterparts, are basically *African* cities, with a few exceptions such as Kaduna. While their growth has been stimulated by the development of foreign-owned businesses, they have never had any significant number of European residents, and many were in existence long before contacts with European civilization—Kumasi, Kano, Ibadan, Abeokuta, Benin, and others. Thus they developed in large measure without European concepts of private property ownership, title registry, surveys, and the like. While some aspects of these features were introduced later, they have never reached the high stage of development found in East Africa. Property titles are often obscure, and there are in many instances no sharp, clearly defined distinctions between private and community ownership, or between leasehold and free-hold. Boundaries are not surveyed and specified. The extended family system is a further source of complication with respect to property rights. In some areas—as, for example, Kumasi and the cities of Northern Nigeria—all land is technically owned by the Crown. In small urban centers, as in the rural areas, communal ownership is common. Consequently, the development of taxation on land has been very slow, and the property taxes have tended to concentrate on buildings.[3]

Ghana

In the last decade, and particularly in the last four years, the Ghana government has made a strong effort to improve local property taxation by encouraging the urban councils to introduce the tax, and by improving the process of valuation. The major characteristics of the present Ghana property rate system include the application of the tax to buildings only, and the taxation of capital values based on reproduction cost less depreciation.

The basis of the present taxation is contained in the Local Government Act, 1961, which provides a single act for cities (Accra), the municipalities (Kumasi, Cape Coast, and Takoradi), and the urban and local councils, consolidating the previous separate

[3] A system of rents for use of tribal or Crown land has developed very slowly, also.

legislation. The Act authorizes the levying by any type of council of an annual rate on the "owner of any premises" (together with the power to levy per capita or graduated personal taxes, and taxes on possessions). Rates may be applied only to property of value in excess of £5. Prior to enactment of this legislation, the four municipal councils had levied a rate based on annual rent of buildings, net of repairs. Whereas vacant land was not taxed, some elements of site value entered into the taxable rental figures. On the other hand, a group of urban councils under authorization of 1951 and 1954 legislation taxed real property on the basis of one tenth of reproduction cost, with an annual rate of 5s. to 6s. on the pound. Eight of these levies had been approved by the government, but two had in practice broken down through inability to effect collections. There was substantial dissatisfaction with these two systems, and recommendations for change were made in the *Report of the Commissioner for Local Government Enquiries* in 1957,[4] and the report of an Australian valuation expert (J. F. N. Murray), obtained through the assistance of the U.N. Technical Assistance Administration.[5]

The Murray report analyzed the difficulties in the various possible approaches to property rating in terms of the circumstances in Ghana—particularly the confused situation of property ownership, with a mixture of private and communal systems, the lack of adequate registry of titles, the confusion on property boundaries, and the absence of any organized market in real estate. The lack of a market rendered unsatisfactory any definition of value based on sale price (as had been provided for in proposed legislation in 1955 which was never enacted). Thus Murray concluded that the reproduction cost approach was best, since all problems of ascertaining sale price were avoided, as well as boundary and title problems; the person entitled to obtain rent from or to occupy the building was the one liable for taxation. Unlike the rental approach, the reproduction cost approach eliminates all site value elements. Under the taxation-of-rental system the site value would be taxed on improved lots but not on those containing no buildings, thus discouraging the use of land for the best purposes. This recommendation was accepted in the new legislation and regulations (1960 and 1961) which provided the replacement cost basis for all councils that wished to use property rates, allowed depreciation from cost up to 25% in ascertaining taxable value, and provided for taxation of all developments rather than mere structures. A uniform system was provided for all types of councils, but in fact only Accra, the

[4] Accra: Government Printer, 1960.
[5] *Report to the Government of Ghana on Valuation and Rating*, by J. F. N. Murray (mimeo.; Sydney, 1958).

municipaiities, and about 12 urban councils actually were taking advantage of the legislation by 1962. Transition to the new system of valuation was, as of mid-1962, only partially completed; the old replacement cost basis with tax on 10% of the cost, the old annual rental value system, and the new replacement cost basis were all in use.

Perhaps the more important aspect of the new system is the extensive revaluation program. During 1962 attention was centered on Accra, Tema (the new harbor town), and some towns that did not previously have property rates. All valuation work has been taken over by the Ministry of Local Government, which now has some 60 valuation officers, probably more than in any other tropical African country. Most of these are Ghanaians. The government is seeking to bring the total up to 100. The general practice is to take persons completing the twelfth grade and subject them to an intensive training program.

The basic approach in the valuation program is the preparation of a block diagram and the listing of each building in its proper place, as ascertained from a house-to-house check. A card is prepared for each building, the building measured, and a valuation figure applied on the basis of building costs and depreciation of the property. Standard building-cost data are developed from records of contracts and other sources. All buildings are grouped into five classes, and minimum and maximum square-footage cost figures prepared for each. The intent is to keep the valuation up to date by frequent rechecks since valuation is regarded as a continuing, not a once-and-for-all, job.

The tax rates are determined by the local council and approved by the Minister of Local Government. The Minister also exercises control over delinquency, which has been a major problem in the past. Kumasi is estimated to be collecting 75% of its potential property rate revenue, and Accra less than half. Under present programs, the Ghana government plans to suspend various grants if the councils do not hold delinquency to a low level. The councils have the right to occupy and sell the property if tax is not paid (a right not common in African countries); since such a sale is regarded as a family disgrace, some member of the family is almost certain to pay. But in the past the councils have often failed to take effective action. Partly because of the poor collections, the tax has been much less important than the poll tax (which itself is not well administered) as a source of local revenue.

Ghana is the only country covered in this study to attempt any form of national government property tax. As a part of the general austerity measures introduced in 1961 on the recommendations of the English economist Kaldor, a tax was levied on property of value in excess of £50, on buildings only, with a rate of 1s. on the pound on the first £500, and 2s. beyond. The intent was to apply the tax to the municipal valuations, but unfortunately, because the valuation system was in transition, there were three different valuation bases in use. Much confusion prevailed in Accra in regard to this question, but the government sought to use the reproduction cost valuations wherever they existed, applying the tax rate to one twelfth of this amount, and seeking to make its own valuations when they did not already exist. Actually, the tax, designed to reach property income now escaping the income tax, was to be applied initially only in Accra, the three municipalities, and Tamale. In addition to confusion, there was also widespread feeling that the tax was a mistake and that repeal was possible. It is very difficult to justify a national tax that applies only in certain areas, and the tax must obviously be extended or eliminated.

Apart from this attempt to use a national tax, the newly developing property rate system has much merit. A professional assessment program will greatly improve equity, and while the reproduction-cost-less-depreciation basis has obvious defects, it may be the only solution in light of the general environment of land ownership and titles. The failure of the community to recover for itself the rising site value of land, either through rates or rents, is unfortunate, but no immediate shift to include land is feasible. Also, the reproduction cost basis inevitably discriminates against persons owning properties which do not have use or sale value equivalent to reproduction cost. But, in fact, some downward grading of valuation is likely in such instances. Inevitably, the taxation of buildings, but not land, may encourage persons to hold land idle and discourage building development—but this is no more characteristic of the reproduction cost approach than others which concentrate the tax on improvements.

Nigeria

Nigeria, with its federal governmental structure and widely varied political, economic, social, and religious backgrounds, has much greater diversity in practice in the taxation of property, and has on the whole failed to develop such taxation to the extent found in Ghana. As of 1962, the property rate program is well developed in Lagos, and of minor consequence elsewhere; Ibadan and Abeokuta, which are two of the largest African cities, have no property rating at all. Rating is facilitated in Lagos by a relatively good property title and registry system, whereas in Eastern and Western Nigeria the title situation is, for the most part, chaotic, with the same mixture of communal and private ownership that prevails in Ghana. In Northern Nigeria, on the other hand, all land is Crown land, and the record systems of occupancy would appear to be much more satisfactory. Just as the British took all Kumasi land for the Crown after the final defeat of the Asantahene, so they declared all Northern Nigeria land to be Crown land after Lord Lugard's defeat of the Emirs.

Valuation for Lagos is carried out by the valuation unit in the Federal Ministry of Lagos Affairs. The unit, which in 1962 had 26 inspectors and valuation officers, also provides assistance for valuation units in the three regions. There has been some discussion of placing the valuation work of all regions in the hands of the Federal unit, but considerable opposition is likely, particularly in Western Nigeria—given the present political situation. Valuation is based upon a somewhat antiquated ordinance of 1916, carried over from the United Kingdom, which is likely to be redrafted in the near future. Under the law, complete revaluation must be made every five years, but lack of adequate personnel has resulted in a two-year delay. Interim changes are made by Lagos City personnel rather than by the Federal staff. Appeals from assessments go to a valuation court of experts. The list of valuations established (some 40,000 parcels) is available for public inspection for 21 days after completion of the roll.

The Lagos property rates are based on annual value, defined as the "rent at which any tenement (building) might reasonably be expected to let, under the assumption that the tenant pays the rates and taxes and the landlord pays the costs of repairs and insurance." Public utility property is, however, assessed on the basis of depreciated capital value. The tax is imposed upon the owner, not the occupier. The aim is to ascertain the rental which would be charged under normal supply-demand conditions, not the actual rental in each case. Property is grouped into four classes (residential, shops, industrial, special), and rental values per square foot built up for various types within each class, for various areas of the city, from data of actual rentals. For industrial and special property (e.g., service stations, theaters) a percentage-of-cost figure is used in reaching the rental value. Unimproved land is not taxed, but no effort is made to remove the site value element from building rents. Lists of property are prepared by the inspectors on a street-by-street basis.

The Lagos rate has been in recent years 9/4 on the pound of annual rental, or $46\frac{2}{3}\%$, a relatively high rate. The rate is not subject to frequent change. The major problem with the tax is delinquency, with the current rate about 20%. Some delinquency takes the form of deliberate evasion; a store owner will obtain a ten-year single-advance-payment lease and then leave the country. He cannot be reached, and there is no means of collecting from the tenant, because the rent is not being paid currently. The law does not permit the seizure of real property for delinquency; civil suit and seizure of movable property are possible, but often no such property can be found.

In Western Nigeria, use is made of property rates only by Sapele and Warri. In Sapele the ratable value is 10% of the capital value, and the rate is 6s. on the pound for residential and 12s. on the pound for nonresidential buildings. Thus there are no rates in the suburbs of Lagos which extend beyond the boundaries (these areas also lack adequate zoning control and include some of the worst slums in all of Africa), in Abeokuta, or in Ibadan. One reason for the limited use is the relative adequacy of local revenues from the income tax.

In Northern Nigeria, legislation makes possible the use of property rates, but in practice their use has been limited to the "township" areas of the three major cities—Kano, Jos, and Zaria—plus Kaduna. The township areas are those which contain the commercial developments and higher-income housing. They are separate governmental units, and are not under the jurisdiction of the Native Authorities. Valuation is performed by the valuation unit of the Lands and Surveys Ministry of Northern Nigeria rather than by the local governments. The annual rental value basis is now being used; capital cost has been used in the past in Kaduna, but the shift is being made to the annual basis. The present rates are 10s. on the pound in Kano, 7s. in Jos, and 5s. in Zaria.

The valuation unit also values land for rental purposes. All land is owned by the Crown, and occupiers in the newer areas are charged ground rents. In the older portions of the cities, persons have traditional rights of occupancy, and no rents are charged (and no property rates are applied).

In Eastern Nigeria somewhat greater use is made of property rates, which are found in eight cities, at rates from 2s. to 4s. (low by comparison with Lagos), based on annual rental value, and applied to buildings only. Valuation has been the responsibility of the local councils, which have employed building inspectors to do the work. Undervaluation has been common, and the general task of valuation has been performed in an unsatisfactory fashion. The regional government valuation office has been largely advisory; the government, however, is seeking to transfer all valuation to the regional office and undertake a complete revaluation of all property in the cities using the tax, if possible with aid from the Federal valuation unit and the U.N. Technical Assistance Board. Rapid growth of the towns and the inadequacy of the per capita personal taxes have increased interest in a more satisfactory property rate system. The cities are also plagued by delinquency, many councils failing to take necessary civil action to obtain payment.

In general, the inadequacy of the existing property rate program except for Lagos is widely recognized, and the urgent need for additional government revenue for development programs is stimulating national interest in gaining additional sums from both property rates and rentals on Crown land. Both represent a source of revenue that is likely to be less detrimental to development than continued increases in other taxes. The major loophole in the system as it stands is the failure to collect rates on unoccupied, privately owned land; not only is the land-speculator favored but building may be discouraged.

Sierra Leone[6]

Property rates are found only in Freetown, the surrounding suburban council areas, and Bo, the country's only other urban center. The Freetown system, with a rate of 3/3 on annual rental value, has improved materially in recent years as a result of complete revaluation in the late fifties by an expert from the United Kingdom. Unfortunately, however, the professional staff was not retained when the revaluation was completed. The suburban areas have very poor-quality and antiquated valuations, and find it difficult to raise adequate revenues. Bo uses a primitive system based simply upon size and type of building, without valuation.

EAST AFRICA

The typical East African practice in the urban property rate field, except for Uganda, is exactly the reverse of that in West Africa; only land is taxed. The taxation of land values in East Africa is of course made possible by the complete system of land registry in the urban areas and the well-defined titles. Actually, most of the land is not held in freehold but on long-term leaseholds, but while this complicates valuation somewhat, it causes no basic difficulty. As in West Africa, however, except for Uganda, the European areas of Kenya, and the very limited plantation areas in Tanganyika, there is little private ownership of farm land, and thus no taxation of such land.

Uganda

The cities of Uganda are relatively small; Kampala has a population of about 50,000, with another 68,000 (mainly Africans) in the surrounding areas; Jinja, 30,000; and Entebbe, 11,000. Kampala,

[6] This section, included for completeness, is based primarily upon the discussion in Mrs. U. K. Hicks's volume *Development from Below* (Oxford: Oxford University Press, 1961).

Jinja, and Mbale are municipalities. Pre-British Uganda was characterized by the complete absence of cities, and even of villages; few areas in Africa had such complete dispersal of population on separate farms. The cities and towns are entirely British creations, although the bulk of the non-African population is Indian. Kampala, Jinja, Mbale, and Masaka levy property rates on the capital values of both land and improvements, with a rate of $1\frac{1}{2}\%$ on the former and $\frac{1}{4}\%$ on the latter. The aim of valuation is full sale value under normal conditions of sale. Revaluation is undertaken every five years. Kampala has its own valuation staff, while valuation for the other three cities is undertaken by the Uganda government valuation unit. With all urban land registered, and with a competent valuation staff, the general assessment standards are good, and few collection problems are encountered in the four cities. The tax yields about 40% of the total revenue and almost all of the tax revenue of the four cities. The basis was shifted from annual rental to sale value during 1947 and 1948; while the new basis is more costly, it has produced more satisfactory results.

There are some 45 smaller towns (including Entebbe) that have been operated as a part of the Uganda government; as of July 1, 1962, 15 of these became autonomous units. These towns tax on an annual value basis only, and assessment has been expensive and frequently unsatisfactory. Some thought is being given to shifting these rates to an arbitrary standard such as square footage to get away from the valuation problem.

Buganda is one of the few jurisdictions in Africa to use a general rural land tax, a practice made possible by the relatively well-defined landownership. There are three rate classes: 1.50s., 5s., and 25s. The landowners are classified by the local assessment committees on the basis of both acreage and quality of the land. The tax is not a major revenue source, yielding in 1961–1962 about £36,000 (compared to £1,250,000 for the graduated personal tax). But it represents a step in the direction of rural land taxation rarely found in Africa.

Kenya

Anyone visiting Nairobi for the first time is inevitably impressed by the modern appearance of the city, even though there has been little building since 1960 as a consequence of uncertainties over the country's economic and political future. Local authorities on the question are convinced that the city's system of applying property rates to land values only has been a major factor in encouraging building, although it is impossible to demonstrate this by any sort of conclusive evidence. Nevertheless, a review of the practice is of particular interest.

There are four types of local governments in Kenya: the six municipalities; the seven county councils in the European areas of the white highlands; the African District Councils, which have jurisdiction over the rural African areas; and the townships, small urban settlements. The counties and ADC units now have the same taxing powers, including the right to levy rates on immovable property, but the ADC's do not use the power, and therefore are not of concern for this discussion; the Kenya government is hopeful that ultimately a system of rural land taxation in the African areas can be developed.

The municipalities have used site value taxation for more than 30 years; apparently its acceptance in East Africa arose out of a spread of ideas of the single tax. This took place shortly after the turn of the century and came from Great Britain through South and Central Africa, and gradually into Kenya. The rates apply to all land except that of the Crown and the East Africa Common Services Organization, which pay sums in lieu of rates.[7] The rates apply to site value only, regardless of the structures on the land. The basis is market value: what the land would sell for if it sold in an open market sale, regardless of the improvements which have actually been made on it. The figures are built up on the basis of all sales figures in the area. Each plot is surveyed and registered, and records of all sales are sent to the valuation office. From these records the standard freehold value per square foot for the particular area is ascertained as a basis for calculating the appropriate valuation for each piece of property in the area. On lands used for specialized purposes such that there are no sales of similar vacant lands, the land value is ascertained by deducting the replacement cost of the improvements from the total value.

The law requires revaluation every five years. In Nairobi, revaluation has occurred every three years, made by an expert valuation staff, which includes four valuation experts, three assistants, clerical and drafting personnel. Interim changes are made only for new subdivisions or unusual circumstances. The valuation is made as of a certain date (and interim changes are all dated back to this figure) and retained, except for interim changes, until the next general valuation. All valuation figures must be approved by the Valuation Court (made up of experts) before they become effective.

The tax rate, currently 2%, is set by the city council, and not subjected to frequent change. While the real property cannot be seized for payment of tax, few delinquency problems are encountered, except occasionally with vacant lots. Property cannot be sold until the tax is paid, and thus ultimate collection is assured.

[7] On the city-owned African estates providing housing for Africans, a rate element is presumably included in the rent; no rates, as such, are paid.

The tax currently yields Nairobi about £885,000 a year, the bulk of the city's tax revenue, and about 45% of its total revenue.

While, on the whole, the system appears to function very satisfactorily, certain problems are encountered:

1. How far back should improvement items be regarded as suitable for exclusion—e.g., original grading? A rule-of-thumb breaking point is used.

2. Should roads be considered improvements, and thus the effects of new streets in increasing values be ignored? The answer is "no"; only improvements to property itself are excluded.

3. How can leasehold values be converted to freehold values, which are the intended base of the tax? In fact, most of the titles are leasehold from the Crown. Conversion is made on the basis of the number of years of the lease. Questions arise, however, about the appropriate interest rate.

4. Whereas the value is supposed to be the figure free from encumbrances, the latter figure is often not easily ascertainable.

5. Questions arise about the ratable unit, particularly of unsold lots in subdivisions; if each is treated separately, the value may be greater in total than it would be if each is treated individually.

6. Most of the industrial land in Nairobi is owned by the government or the railway and is not sold outright; thus special valuation problems are created.

The site value basis is regarded as highly satisfactory by city officials and the city councils; Kenya legislation permits the application of rates to improvements as well, but the council prefers the land value basis, under the strong conviction that the system is largely responsible for the very rapid growth and modernization of the city. The other major advantage is the greater simplicity of valuing land over valuing improvements. Thus, a smaller staff is feasible.

The townships, which are of minor importance, also typically apply rates to site value, with valuation by the Kenya government.

In the county council areas, the site value basis is also permitted and is generally used in the urban areas, as, for example, the suburban areas around Nairobi. In the rural areas, however, this basis is not used, the county councils employing one of various alternative, authorized methods. One is a flat sum per acre, the total often graduated in a regressive fashion according to the number of acres owned. A typical rate schedule is as follows: up to a 20-acre holding, 2s. per acre; 20–50 acres, 1.50s. per acre; 50–100 acres, 1s.; 100–500 acres, 60¢; beyond 500 acres, 10¢. In other council areas, land is classified by use (farm, pastoral, etc.) and a flat rate assessed for each type. The rates are low, reflecting the fact that the county councils actually perform relatively few functions.

Zanzibar

Property rates are used by the municipality of Zanzibar, with a 10% tax on annual gross value; in 1960 this tax yielded about 33% of total municipal revenue, and virtually all the tax revenue. Tax does not apply to indigenous housing, and thus two thirds of the population are completely exempt. There is no expert valuation staff. When property is rented, the actual gross rent is taken as the basis; when the property is occupied by the owner, 5% of the capital value is taken as the rental figure. Vacant land (of which there is very little) is theoretically taxable but in fact is frequently not reached. There is no title registry system except for transfer of buildings, and no cadastral survey or real proof of the ownership of land. In 1961, a complete revaluation was undertaken, the first in 25 years. Although most farm land is privately owned, there is no title registry or survey and no attempt to use a land tax.

Tanganyika

In the last decade, the Tanganyika cities have followed the Kenya system of taxing site value only; most of the city councils have, of course, been set up only since 1955. Prior to that year, a relatively crude house tax was the only form of urban property tax. Tanganyika has one major city, Dar es Salaam, and 11 autonomous urban councils; other urban local governments are operated by the Tanganyika government through appointed councils.

In Dar es Salaam and the urban council areas, property rates are applied to the unimproved land values only, and thus improvements are not subject to tax. Whereas taxation of improvements is authorized by legislation (subject to the approval of the Minister of Local Government), this action has not been taken, because of the desire to encourage building. The tax rates are set by the city councils subject to approval of the Minister; the Dar es Salaam rate is 2.6%, the others ranging from 2.5 to 3.5%.

Revaluation is undertaken at five-year intervals with annual supplements, and all valuation is made by the Tanganyika government valuation unit in the Ministry of Land and Surveys. Most property is held on a leasehold basis, the valuations being converted to freehold. Those on a leasehold of fewer than five years are not taxed to the leaseholder; instead, the government (as the owner) pays, and presumably includes the amount in the rent charged.

In addition to the site value tax, there is also imposed an urban house tax, required of all persons occupying houses located on sites on which the owners do not pay property rates. Thus, in fact, this tax reaches the numerous "squatters" on government land. The rates vary with location, ranging from 20s. to 300s. There is no attempt at valuation, but houses are grouped into rate classes according to location. This tax replaced a levy known as the local government tax, which had also been designed to require payment of some tax by residents who did not pay tax on land which they owned. The rate was the difference between the amount paid by the person in local property rate and the amount of the personal tax in the area surrounding the city.

In the nonautonomous urban areas, instead of site value rates, there is imposed an urban "house" tax on all buildings, levied as a percentage of annual rental value, defined as gross rental less 10%. There is no tax on unimproved land. The rates, typically 10%, and limited to 15%, are set locally, subject to the approval of the Minister of Local Government. The assessments are made by a local assessment committee consisting of three local officials. Revaluation is undertaken every three years.

Enforcement problems vary; some of the smaller town councils are seriously in arrears because of their failure to press for payment of delinquent taxes. The same problem arises as in Nairobi, namely that of finding the owners of some vacant property. The law does not permit the seizure and sale of real property for failure to pay taxes, but the tax constitutes a lien against the property, and the owner can be sued in court.

CENTRAL AFRICA

In all three territories of the Federation of Rhodesia and Nyasaland, the same basic policy is followed on property rates: both improvements and land values are taxed, but the latter at a much higher rate, in fact, often four to six times as high. There are seven cities in the Federation with populations of 50,000 or more: Salisbury (283,000); Bulawayo (202,000), Kitwe (83,000), Lusaka (80,000), Ndola (79,000), Luanshya (60,000), and Blantyre (50,000). The first two are in Southern Rhodesia, Blantyre in Nyasaland, and the others in Northern Rhodesia. In all instances the African element is the largest, but Salisbury, with almost 100,000 Europeans, has one of the largest European populations in Africa outside of South Africa. Salisbury is one of the most modern cities in the world, and has experienced very rapid growth since 1945.

In predominately rural Nyasaland, the town councils use property rates, applied to the capital value of land and buildings, with a higher rate on land than on buildings.

In Northern Rhodesia, with its substantial number of medium-sized cities (most, except Lusaka, are mining towns), property rates are of substantial importance, the gross ratable value in 1960 being £109 million (£22 million, land; £87 million, improvements). The rates are employed in 23 urban communities. The local councils set the rates; all tax both land and improvements, but with a substantial differential. Examples include (land rate first): Lusaka 2s., 10d.; Ndola, 1¾s., 6½d.; Kitwe, 2s., 5½d. The highest rate on improvements is 2½s. and the lowest, ½s.; the highest on land, 10d. and the lowest, 2½d. The higher rate on land is designed to discourage land speculation and to aid building development. Rate increases must receive the approval of the Minister of Local Government. African housing areas are not currently subject to the rate and for the most part are owned by the local governments.

The aim of the legislation is to apply the rate to actual freehold sale value, i.e., the value as a freehold even if it is not one at the figure the property would sell for in a normal free market. When the title is a leasehold, no adjustment is made. Valuation is made by the valuation unit in the Ministry of Local Government, except in Lusaka, which has its own valuation officer. After valuation is completed, the roll is made available for public inspection; anyone objecting can appeal to the resident magistrate, and an independent appraiser is appointed. Complete revaluation is undertaken every five years, with interim adjustments. The tax is a levy on the owner.

In valuation, the normal approach is to maintain a record of all actual sales as a basis for building up the value figures for each type of property. The land-only sales serve as a basis for determining the value of the land in the particular section, and the land for each parcel is determined independently of whether there is a building on it or not. Then the over-all values of the land and improvements are determined on the basis of sales figures, and land values are subtracted to get the improvement values. These figures are then reduced to a square-footage basis to provide the standard for valuation. On business property, however, the rental figure is regarded as the best guide to ascertain the sale value figure of the property as a whole. Valuation is facilitated by lists and building plans of new buildings which are kept by the municipalities; by complete registry of all deeds; and by records of land sales. All buildings which are assessed are inspected.

Unpaid tax constitutes a civil debt, and court action can be taken; after three years, the municipality can enter into possession of the property.

The Southern Rhodesia property rate system is much the same, the property rates being confined to the urban areas and applied to both land and improvements, with a substantially higher rate on the former. In addition, rural road councils in the European areas levy a flat sum of tax against each piece of property, regardless of size, for road purposes. Salisbury and Bulawayo have their own valuation units, and valuation in the remaining municipalities is performed by the Southern Rhodesia government valuation office. The procedure described below is that of Bulawayo, but the others are not basically different.

Revaluation is required by law every ten years but in fact is made every three years. Every six months an interim set of changes is made for new buildings and other instances where substantial change has occurred in particular values; the law does not permit interim revaluation in other cases. The listing of properties, of which there are about 9,000 in Bulawayo, is prepared from information in the deeds registry office, and the details on new buildings are provided by the building plans, copies of which are sent to the valuation office. Figures for valuation are developed from cost data on new construction and from sales figures of existing properties.

The aim of valuation is the sale price in an open-market transaction, that is, 100% of sale value. However, the actual approach varies. Frequently, the property as a whole is valued, the value of the land ascertained, and the value of improvements calculated by subtracting the land value from the total. Standard figures per acre and per square foot are then ascertained and used as the basis for valuation, subject to modification in particular instances. On business area property, the most suitable approach is found to be the capitalization of net rents; the value of the land is then deducted to find the value of the improvements. On residential and industrial property the more common approach is via the calculation of reproduction cost less depreciation. On special properties, such as cinemas, the volume of business is a major element which is considered in determining value figures.

On the general valuations, inspectors carefully examine all properties, checking on plans, nature of structure, gardens, etc. The valuation is then made, and the valuation officer checks over the property quickly, since he has all measurements and other details supplied to him. A notice is left for the taxpayer; if he objects to the figure, he appears before the Valuation Court, whose decision is final. Appeal is uncommon; there were only nine appeals from 9,000 valuations in the last general roll.

There are few problems of delinquency. Much of the tax is paid in conjunction with mortgage payments.

CONCLUDING OBSERVATIONS

Out of this review of practice in tropical Africa, several concluding comments are in order:

1. Despite the relatively early stage of economic development of these countries, high standards of valuation are encountered in the urban areas. Unlike the United States in the comparable period of development, valuation for property tax purposes is regarded as a task to be performed by experts. Over-all standards of valuation appear to be high, and something approaching full-value assessment, with frequent reassessments, is attained. This is as true of the African cities of Ghana, plus Lagos and Northern Nigeria, as it is of "white" Southern Rhodesia.

2. The capital value approach appears to be far more satisfactory for developing economies than the annual rental basis, and continued use of the latter in Nigeria is a carry-over from British practice, which leaves much to be desired. With the rental basis, improvements lead to immediate tax increases, and the taxes are tied to existing buildings rather than potential ones.

3. The application of the tax to land values only is regarded as highly satisfactory and a significant aid to building development in East Africa. Certainly it would appear that this approach not only restricts land speculation but also aids building development. However, as pointed out by Mrs. Hicks, there are certain limitations. There is danger that too much capital will flow into buildings as a consequence, and less into other forms of economic development; there is some indication that this has occurred in Salisbury, which is one of the world's most attractive cities but is rather obviously overbuilt in terms of the country's needs. Exclusive reliance on this approach concentrates the burden of additional services on landowners, whereas the construction of new buildings may be largely responsible for costs of additional municipal services. Practical limitations on the potential height of site value rates may impair the ability of a city to provide additional and needed municipal services. Moreover, as a city grows, a technical problem is encountered; there may be very few sales of vacant land, and valuation of the land becomes difficult. Nevertheless, the approach, properly employed, has great merit.

4. A major obstacle to effective use of urban property rates on land in West Africa, especially Nigeria, is the unsatisfactory system of land titles and registry. Reform of the title situation would contribute much to property taxation and to other aspects of economic development, but is not a step which can be taken overnight. Meanwhile, the concentration of the tax on buildings, the reverse of the East African procedure, may hinder construction; one of the most urgent needs of the typical West African city is better housing. This same difficulty prevents suitable use of land taxation in agricultural areas, yet there is need for such taxation as

more and more African farmers rise above subsistence levels and as land values rise.[8]

5. When land is owned by the Crown or local community, an effective program of rental charges for the use of the land is essentially the same as a program of land value rates under freehold or long-term leasehold ownership of property. While Northern Nigeria and a few other areas have sought to develop suitable rental charges for use of Crown land in limited urban areas, none has developed a systematic program for wider areas.

6. Governments of developing economies face a major problem of finding adequate revenues to finance development programs in the face of low per capita incomes, which limit severely the yield of all taxes. There is thus the danger that taxes may be driven to levels which will impede economic growth by their adverse incentive effects and in this way destroy the effectiveness of the over-all program. Under such circumstances, further development of land taxation, both urban and rural, offers major potentialities for providing needed funds without impairing incentives. Such taxes will also recapture for society a portion of the gains from increases in land values and provide more equitable tax treatment of farmers, who tend to escape income taxation until a very high stage of economic development is reached. Unlike taxes on output of farm land, taxes on land values will encourage better utilization of the land. In urban areas, while confining property taxes to land offers certain advantages, ultimate partial application to buildings may be essential in terms of revenue and provision of equitable distribution of charges for additional government services. On the whole, improved property taxation may prove to be one of the most profitable avenues of approach to fiscal problems of economic growth.

SELECTED REFERENCES

Hicks, U. K., *Development from Below*. Oxford: Oxford University Press, 1961.

Wald, H. P., *Taxation of Agricultural Land in Underdeveloped Economies*. Cambridge: Harvard University Press, 1959.

Murray, J. F. N., *Report to the Government of Ghana on Valuation and Rating* (mimeo.). Sydney, Australia, 1958.

Lund, F., "Valuation for Rating in Northern Rhodesia." *Journal of Association of Rating and Valuation Officers*, 1956.

[8] In some jurisdictions the taxation of the product of the farm land is regarded as a substitute for the taxation of the land itself. The tax, known as a "cess," which reached general use in Kenya and Tanganyika and is used to a limited extent in some other countries, is usually collected on basic crops sold through controlled markets. The taxes can be very lucrative sources of revenue, but they have potentially serious adverse effects on production, just as do the export taxes.

8 Financing Federation

O NE OF THE MOST PRESSING PROBLEMS in any federal governmental system is that of the allocation of revenue sources, and particularly taxes, between the federal and subordinate governments. Thus, the experience on this issue in the newly developed federations in Africa is of particular interest. One of the major questions is that of the extent to which the new federations have been able to avoid some of the difficulties of the older ones, difficulties arising from features which were introduced generations ago and are highly resistant to change.

Two of the eight countries have truly federal structures—Nigeria and the Federation of Rhodesia and Nyasaland. The three countries of British East Africa—Kenya, Uganda, and Tanganyika—have no central federal government but do have a number of features of a federal structure, so far as taxation is concerned. Nigeria, Rhodesia, and East Africa have certain characteristics in common—a small number (three) of subordinate units, a relatively early stage of economic development, with heavy reliance on primitive agriculture, a common language, British traditions and institutions of government, and formation as a federal state within the last three decades.

THE FEDERATION OF RHODESIA AND NYASALAND

The Federation of Rhodesia and Nyasaland, often referred to as the "Central African Federation," and in southern Africa generally as the "Federation," consists of three previously separate territories: Nyasaland, Northern Rhodesia, and Southern Rhodesia. The backgrounds of the three are very different. Nyasaland is small in area but with a population comparable to that of the others, about 2.85 million people, of whom only 9,000 are Europeans. Once thinly settled, it has grown rapidly in population since 1900, largely by emigration from Portuguese East Africa, and is now relatively overpopulated. Nyasaland was made a British protectorate in 1892, largely to keep out the Portuguese. A beautiful country of mountains, rivers, and lakes, it has relatively few resources and by far the lowest per capita income in the Federation.

Northern Rhodesia, vast in area but in large measure consisting of uninhabitable desert, has about 2.5 million people, of whom about 80,000 are Europeans—mostly farmers along the railway line, and miners in the north. While much of Northern Rhodesia is poor, its wealth in copper ore is of great importance to the country as a whole, and it provides most of the foreign exchange. Northern Rhodesia was ruled by the British South Africa Company until 1924; in that year it became a protectorate, with a legislative council controlled by the appointed government officials and thus by the Colonial Office. The white settler element long sought greater control of the country.

Southern Rhodesia, with 3.1 million persons, is the most populous of the three territories and contains the two major cities, Salisbury and Bulawayo. With 225,000 Europeans, Southern Rhodesia has the largest white population of any African country between South Africa and the Sahara. The area came under control of the South Africa Company largely by virtue of conquest of the Matabele and the Mashona in the 1890's. Political power gradually passed into the hands of the settlers, and in 1923, Southern Rhodesia was formally annexed to the Crown as a self-governing colony, almost, but not quite, with dominion status. Industrial development in Southern Rhodesia has been rapid, together with expansion of tobacco and other agricultural production. Economically, the two Rhodesias were tied together by the railway that was built northward from a connection with the South African system, through Bechuanaland to Bulawayo and on to the copper country, completed in 1909. Nyasaland, however, is separated from the Rhodesias in its populous southern part by Mozambique, and the only rail connection is the long route via Dondo and Umtali.

120

Thus the Federation has a total of about 8 million people, some 300,000 of whom are European, plus about 25,000 Asians (largely from India). Per capita income of the Europeans is one of the highest in the world—about £580 per capita, or £2,320 per family (about $6,500 a year per family). On the other hand, the African per capita income is estimated at £24, less than that of Uganda (£26), for example.

Establishment of the Federation

Thought had been given to possible federation or amalgamation for a number of years, and in 1938, a royal commission was appointed to investigate the question. The commission recommended against such action because of the divergencies among the territories and African opposition in the two northern territories to closer ties, but sought the establishment of a council to attain coordination of various services. This recommendation was accepted in 1945. In 1950, the British government again raised the question of some form of union among the three territories. Various conferences were held on the question, and despite substantial African opposition, a Federation was brought into force in September, 1953. While the change had considerable support in the country, mainly on the part of the Europeans, the impetus came from the British government, not from any strong pressure from the population of the territories as a whole.

Significant powers were transferred to the Federation government, thus necessitating the provision of substantial revenues. The task of drafting a revenue proposal was given to a Fiscal Commission established for the purpose, headed by Sir Jeremy Raisman (who has subsequently headed somewhat similar commissions in East Africa and Nigeria), but made up primarily of civil servants, not of experts in the field of public finance. The terms of reference, so far as taxation was concerned, required that the Commission consider how the revenues available could best be collected and distributed to the four governments, in view of the need for (1) autonomy of the constituent territories, and (2) ensuring that revenues were employed for the benefit of the Federation as a whole. The terms of reference included the question of the best form of income taxation to ensure uniformity throughout the area, and the establishment of a customs union. The Commission's basic approach was to estimate the expenditures by each government and then ascertain the pattern of allocation of revenue which would cover the expenditures, consistent with the other requirements. Out of the recommendations of the Commission came the system still in operation (with minor changes) until the end of 1963.

Allocation of Taxing Powers

In general, the system involved the establishment of a very high degree of centralization of taxation in the hands of the Federation —much more than is typical in non-African federal government structures. The major elements are as follows:

1. Customs and excises. The establishment of a customs union and thus a common market was regarded as essential and, in fact, a major advantage of federation. Previously, each territory had its own customs system. The tariff in Nyasaland and that for a portion of Northern Rhodesia had no Commonwealth preference because of the terms of the Congo Basin Treaty. The Southern Rhodesia tariff was based on that of South Africa; in fact, the two countries were close to a customs union. For the Federation, a single customs system similar to that of Southern Rhodesia was recommended and accepted. All customs and excise revenue was assigned to the Federation government, with one exception. The duty on motor fuel (or an alternative tax on the sale), though administered by the Federation, is subject to the jurisdiction of the territories so far as rates are concerned, and the revenue accrues to them. The main reason for this exception was that the tax in Southern Rhodesia was high and yielded substantial revenue, while there was great opposition in Northern Rhodesia to raising its rate to a similar level.

2. Income tax. Substantial importance was attached to the need for a single national income tax, uniform in structure throughout the country, the prevention of any form of double taxation by the territories, and the avoidance of nuisance for the taxpayer and of duplicating administration. Yet the territories obviously required revenue from this tax. Thus several features were provided:

    a. A single unified income tax structure, with assessment and collection of the tax by the Federal government.

    b. The distribution of the revenue among the four governments, on the basis of a formula derived from an estimate of expenditure needs and revenues from other sources. The Federal government was assigned 60%, Southern and Northern Rhodesia each 17%, and Nyasaland 6%. It was recognized that the formula would not be suitable indefinitely, and provision for reconsideration was included in the recommendations.

    c. The privilege for the territories to add a surcharge to the Federation tax, up to the amount of 20%, in order to give more autonomy and flexibility to the territories. Liability for the surcharge is based on residence for individuals, and territory of origin of the income of companies.

    d. Substantial progression in the income tax structure. The use of the tax structure of the Southern Rhodesian levy (which had been based on the South African tax) was recommended and adopted; there was little progression in the Northern Rhodesia tax.

The net effect of the acceptance of these provisions was to give to the Federation power over income taxation far greater than is typical in other federations—Nigeria, Canada, the United States, and Switzerland, for example—and thus to restrict the taxing powers of the regions materially.

3. Export duties. These had been used only by Nyasaland, and it was assumed that they would not be used by the Federation. But the Commission recognized that they could be used to undercut the income tax. If imposed on exports whose prices are determined in world markets, they reduce the net taxable incomes of the producers. Thus the Commission recommended that any revenues from this source be allocated on the same formula as the income tax.

4. Sales tax. The Commission noted the potential effects of sales taxes on excise and income tax revenue, and the dangers of their interfering with trade across territorial lines. Thus, it recommended that they be exclusively under federal jurisdiction, with revenue allocated on a formula basis, the Federation not to receive more than one third.

Operation of the System

The single unified customs tariff and income tax law were brought into effect.[1] However, motor fuel levies of the three territories vary widely. The three territories all levied surcharges up to the maximum 20% on income tax with one exception: Northern Rhodesia does not impose a surcharge on the personal income tax. There are several reasons: the high yield of the company tax surcharge, the widespread discontent in Northern Rhodesia with federation, and the desire to attract outside investment.

No sales tax has been introduced, largely because of the fears of collection difficulties at the retail level, and the obvious disadvantages of the other possible levels.

As the system operated in the 1961–1962 fiscal year, the Federation collected £43 million for its own use, and an additional £28 million for the territories, whereas the latter themselves collected only £8.7 million of tax revenue. The revenues are shown in Table 8.1.

[1] In 1957, the allocation figures were changed to give the Federation 62%, Southern Rhodesia 14%, Northern Rhodesia 18%, and Nyasaland 6%.

TABLE 8.1   TAX REVENUES, FEDERATION OF RHODESIA AND
NYASALAND, BUDGET ESTIMATES, 1961–1962,
IN THOUSANDS OF POUNDS

Tax	Nyasa-land	South-ern Rho-desia	North-ern Rho-desia	Terri-tories Total	Federa-tion	Total
Centrally Collected:						
Income Tax	2,480	5,753	7,377	15,610	26,089	48,953
Income Tax,						
Surcharge	200	3,000	4,054	7,254	—	—
Customs and						
Excise	241	4,800	225	5,266	17,225	22,491
Total	2,921	13,553	11,656	28,130	43,314	71,444
Collected by Territories:						
Personal Tax	1,055	2,500	345	3,900		3,900
Other	195	3,892	730	4,817		4,817
Total	1,250	6,392	1,075	8,717		8,717
Total	4,171	19,945	12,731	36,847	43,314	80,161

Thus the income tax, including the territorial surcharge, is by far the most important element in the tax structure, yielding 60% of the over-all revenues—a most unusual situation in a developing economy. Since the Federation collects both income taxes and customs and excise, it collects, in total, 76% of the territorial revenues and 89% of the total revenue of all four governments. The personal tax and motor vehicle and other license taxes are the principal levies collected by the territories.

Merits and Complaints

The system obviously has important advantages, which can easily be overlooked. Discriminatory double taxation of interterritorial income is completely avoided, as well as nuisance for taxpayers of varying territorial tax structures and the need for filing duplicating tax returns. In fact, complete uniformity of income taxation is attained, except for the absence of a surtax on individual incomes in Northern Rhodesia. The Federation government has, in effect, complete control over most of the total tax revenue and thus is placed in a particularly good position to adjust taxation for purposes of attaining greater economic stability. Nuisance features of differing commodity taxation in the various jurisdictions are avoided (except on motor fuel). Allocation to the territories of much of the revenue by a prearranged formula gives some recognition to varying revenue needs and avoids the problem of ascertaining origin of the revenue.

However, this efficiency in operation has been attained at the price of substantial loss of fiscal autonomy on the part of the territories, and, particularly in Nyasaland and Southern Rhodesia, there is a strong feeling on the part of the territorial governments that they have inadequate total revenues to finance the functions assigned to them. The major source, the income tax, is dependent in its yield strictly on Federation policy, completely so far as the shared portion is concerned, and actually with the surcharges as well, since the latter have, with the exception noted, been held at the maximum. Adjustments in the Federation income tax automatically produce changes in the major revenues of the territories, and these adjustments are apparently made with little consulation with the territories; the Federation determines its tax policy largely on its own. The territories are left with only minor autonomous revenues, and one of these, the motor fuel tax, is administered by the Federation. In Southern Rhodesia, there has been a tendency to use the motor fuel tax as the balancing item in the budget, whereas under usual principles of taxation this levy is particularly unsuited for the purpose. The territories are of course permitted to levy personal or poll taxes, and all three do so. But these taxes cannot raise significant sums of revenue without violating usual standards of equity unless they are graduated, and in the past the territories have concluded that graduation would render the taxes invalid by giving them the form of income taxes, which are within the Federation's sphere. In 1961, however, Southern Rhodesia introduced limited graduation into its tax. But at best these can only be minor revenue sources.

Northern Rhodesia's principal criticism is of a slightly different nature. With the large profits of the mining industry in the territory, Northern Rhodesia, in a sense, subsidizes the other two territories by paying a disproportionate share of Federation tax, although, on the whole, Southern Rhodesia is much the wealthier area.

There is also criticism, especially in Nyasaland, of the high exemptions under the personal income tax, which are attributed to the desire of the Federation government to attract European immigrants.

The Monckton Recommendations

In 1960, a complete review of the Constitution of the Federation was undertaken by a group generally known from the name of its chairman as the Monckton Commission. The Commission recommended a substantial redistribution of governmental functions, and the establishment of a Fiscal Commission to reallocate the proceeds of taxation among the four governments. Two general principles were emphasized, so far as taxation is concerned: the range of taxes under the control of the territories should be as wide as possible, yet the Federation government should be able to exercise broad fiscal policy to aid in stabilization of the economy. It was recognized, of course, that these two goals were somewhat contradictory. The principal change recommended was the allocation of customs duties on the basis of a prescribed formula, in order to increase the revenues of the territories in conformity with their enlarged functions. No basic changes in the income tax were suggested, except that the maximum of the surcharge be stated in terms of tax rate rather than a percentage of the Federation tax, so that the territorial yield would not move automatically with changes in the Federation levy. In addition, authorization for the territories to institute graduated poll taxes (but with no overlap of liability for poll and income tax) was recommended.

The Monckton Commission also reviewed the question of whether the power for determining income tax rates should rest with the Federation or territorial governments, and offered two alternatives: (1) that the present system continue; and (2) that the territories be permitted to fix the rates of the personal income tax, subject to Federation regulation and collection. The basic company tax would remain a Federation tax. No formal preference for either of these was indicated.

Thus, on the whole, the recommended changes would not have drastically altered the present system so far as the levying and collection of taxes were concerned, the main change being allocation among the four governments of the proceeds of the customs duties. Administration and determination of customs and income tax structures would remain Federation functions, as well as rate determination, except for the surcharges, unless the second alternative noted in the previous paragraph was accepted.

The Future

The recommendations of the Monckton report were not implemented. When Nyasaland and Northern Rhodesia gained African governments in 1962 and 1963, they sought the right to withdraw from the Federation because of its domination by "white" Southern Rhodesia. This right was granted by Great Britain in 1963, and a conference at Victoria Falls resolved the major issues relating to dissolution. The Federation is scheduled to end on December 31, 1963. Whether or not a customs union and any sort of joint tax administration will continue has not been resolved as of September, 1963. Meanwhile, ten years of experience with a highly centralized tax system demonstrated its technical efficiency on the one hand and its effects on territorial autonomy on the other.

NIGERIA

Unlike the Central African Federation, Nigeria assumed federal status from a unitary state. The transition was made in order to increase the chances of the country remaining intact after independence. The divergent interests among the three regions were so great that a unitary state appeared almost certain to disintegrate.

The Nature of the Country

Nigeria, like other African countries, did not exist as a unit prior to the coming of the British. British rule was gradually extended northward, and control was completed in 1903. Not until 1914, however, were the northern and southern protectorates united to form the Colony and Protectorate of Nigeria. Self-government came slowly until after World War II, when the movement speeded up rapidly. The 1946 and 1951 constitutions both provided for a unitary state. But quarrels between the North and the South brought a near breakdown in government, and the result was a new constitution in 1953 providing for a federal structure. On the basis of this new constitution Nigeria became independent on October 1, 1960.

The country consists of the Federal district of Lagos (following the United States–Australian pattern), and Eastern, Western, and Northern Nigeria. The North has slightly more than half of the population, the East slightly more than the West. The East and West have some characteristics in common, such as heavily wooded terrain, but also significant differences. The West, dominated by the Yoruba, is characterized by village and city dwelling, and contains some of the oldest African cities—Ibadan, Abeokuta, Ife, and Benin. Tribal rule was typically hereditary. Economically, this area is comparable to Ghana, with its heavy reliance on cocoa. The East, whose relatively small cities are mainly European creations, is a thickly settled land of village and farm dwellings, with production concentrated on palm oil. The dominant tribe is the Ibo, one of the most important democratic tribes of Africa, with no tradition of chiefs or central authority.

The North is a very different type of country, in terms of physical environment, culture, government, religion, and virtually every aspect of life. It is a land of vast semiarid plains, of mud-walled cities dating back to 1000 A.D. (Kano, Zaria, and Katsina are the chief examples), of predominately Moslem culture, of autocratic governments of Emirs and Sultans (but now with a substantial element of democracy), of primitive agricultural methods, but extensive production for market. There were no indigenous ties with the South at all; those which exist, such as the railway lines, were creations of the British.

So far as taxation is concerned, prior to 1952 the regions had no taxing powers of their own, but were assigned arbitrarily allocated shares of Federal revenue. In 1951, some taxing powers were given to the regions, and in the 1954 constitution these were extended, on the basis of the recommendations of Sir Louis Chick, who had served as Revenue Commissioner. Under the 1954 system, revenues of import, excise, and export duties were assigned to the regions on the basis of derivation or by fixed percentage (general customs revenue). Federally collected income tax revenues on companies and on non-Africans were returned to the regions, as were mining royalties. Various produce sales taxes were also used by the regions; purchase taxes on motor fuel, beer, and spirits in the East and taxes on personal income in the Eastern and Western regions.

The Raisman Report

Dissatisfaction with the system led to the appointment of a Fiscal Commission in 1957, consisting of Sir Jeremy Raisman (Chairman) and R. C. Tress. This Commission reviewed the whole question of fiscal arrangements and made a number of suggestions, almost all of which were accepted, and which form the basis of the present tax arrangements. Most of the criticisms of the old system centered around the lack of sufficient autonomous revenues for the regions, the difficulties in the ascertainment of the origin of the revenues from various regions, particularly import duties, and failure to recognize the lack of correlation between the needs of a region and its revenues. The Commission sought to attain an effective compromise between maximum fiscal autonomy on the part of the regions and attainment of administrative effectiveness, free interregional trade (regarded as of utmost importance), and unified national policy, particularly financial stability of the Federal government.

The system developed on the basis of the Raisman report contains the following major elements:

1. Exclusive jurisdiction is given to the Federal government over:

    a. Customs, excise, and export duties.
    b. Sales and purchase taxes, except those on produce (other than tobacco), hides and skins, motor fuel.
    c. Taxes on the income and profits of companies.
    d. Mining royalties and rents.
    e. Taxes on incomes of persons resident in Lagos.

2. The regional governments and their subdivisions, therefore, have the power over:

    a. Personal income taxes, subject to the requirements noted below.

b. Taxes on the sale of the items enumerated in 1*b* above.

c. Poll or graduated personal taxes.

d. Taxes on wealth and property, including real property, livestock, and other possessions.

e. License taxes.

3. Since this allocation provided entirely inadequate funds to the regional governments, yet no additional transfer of taxing powers was considered consistent with the need for free interregional trade and administrative feasibility, provision was made for allocation of certain Federal revenues to the regions.

The allocations are based upon two principles: derivation (that is, where the tax revenue was generated) and need for funds. In terms of these criteria, the allocation system was set up as follows:

a. Exclusively to the regions of origin:

(1) Import duties on motor fuel.

(2) Import and excise duties on tobacco.

(3) Export duties on produce, hides, and skins.

b. Exclusively to the Federal government:

(1) Import duties on beer, wine, and liquor.

(2) Excise duty on beer.

c. Allocated to distributable pool:

(1) 30% of all import duties other than those listed above, the other 70% retained by the Federal government.

(2) 30% of mining rents and royalties; 50% of the revenues go to the region of origin; 20% to the Federal government.

In addition, the company tax and the Lagos personal income tax yields go exclusively to the Federal government.

The distributable pool is allocated as follows: 40/95 to the North; 24/95 to the West; 31/95 to the East.

The allocation system is written into the constitution, and cannot be altered except by action of the legislatures of two regions and Parliament. The constitution also provides that from time to time the Federal government shall appoint a commission to review the allocation, but this has not yet been done.

Income Tax

The Raisman Commission was eager to ensure that, while the setting of personal income tax rates and allowances should rest within the jurisdiction of the regions, at the same time multiple taxation should be avoided. The decision to keep the tax at the regional level, in contrast to the policy in other new federations, was based upon several considerations, in addition to the desire to give the regions as many autonomous revenue sources as possible: the traditional use of direct personal tax by the regions, the need for adapting the tax to local conditions, the importance of direct tax systems in the tax structure of the Native Authorities in the North; and the existing use of income taxation in the East and the West.

To ensure satisfactory operation of the tax system, however, the Federation was given power to enact legislation affecting tax on individual incomes, for the purposes of:

1. Implementing double-taxation treaties with other countries.

2. Securing uniform treatment of international income.

3. Prevention of double taxation of the same income by more than one region.

4. Attainment of uniformity in the computation of taxable income, the treatment of losses, depreciation, and contributions to pension systems.

5. Facilitating arrangements between the regions and the Federal government relating to exemption of certain incomes.

6. Facilitating exchange of information on the income tax by various taxing jurisdictions.

7. Establishment, by cooperation of the various governments, of authorities designed to increase the uniformity of taxation.

However, the Federal government was denied the power to establish tax rates, personal allowances, or reliefs, which were left specifically to the regions. Thus a framework was provided to prevent double taxation and ensure uniformity in the calculation of income, yet to ensure autonomy to the regions so far as level of the tax and treatment of dependents were concerned.

Pursuant to this provision, the Federal government, after consultation with the three regional governments, enacted the Income Tax Management Act in 1961. The Act seeks to prevent double taxation by giving exclusive jurisdiction to the region of residence of the person for the year. The Act also defines income in some detail and specifies the treatment of partnership income, dividends and interest, deductions for calculating taxable income (other than allowances for dependents), losses, depreciation, and the like. Residence is defined in great detail. A Joint Tax Board was established to handle questions of interpretation under the Act, and related matters.

It is by no means clear how far the Federal government can go, constitutionally, in the direction taken in the Income Tax Management Act, and to what extent the Act is actually binding on the regions, since this is a field of concurrent taxing powers. The source of doubt is the fact that, while the Federation is given various powers in the field, at the same time, the constitution guarantees the autonomy of the regions. It would appear that there is no doubt on issues on which the constitution is specific, such as the prevention of double taxation. There is doubt, however, on the question of various deductions authorized by the Act. Must the regions adjust their laws to provide these, or can they fail to grant some allowances provided in the Federal Act? Can they provide additional allowances not given in the Federal Act? The most common answer is that they must provide the allowances mentioned, but may give others. The unofficial reaction in Western Nigeria, however, is that the Act is much less binding on the regions than is usually thought.[2]

Apart from the question of the exact scope of Federal powers over income taxation, there are certain other questions of interpretation that the courts must decide. One is the concept of "produce"; the regions are entitled to apply sales taxes to produce (and a few other items). Does the term include articles manufactured from products grown in the area, or only those in the form of unprocessed or partially processed agricultural goods?

The Revenue Picture

The 1961–1962 Budget Estimates give a general picture of the actual revenue sources under the Federal system as it operates. Lagos is included in the Federal figures.

A few general comments can be made about Table 8.2. The Federal government collects about £85 million in tax revenue annually, the regions about £11 million. However, the Federal government retains only about half of the total, or roughly £44 million. The remainder (£41 million) is transmitted to the regions, which thus get 79% of their total of £52 million of tax revenue from the Federal government. The expenditures from tax revenue of the Federal government and those of the regions, in total, are comparable (£47 million versus £52 million), but the Federal government is the chief tax collector, and the financial autonomy of the regions—despite their freedom to impose personal income taxes—is not actually very great. This situation results in large part from the fact that, given the general nature of the economy, much of the revenue must come from customs duties, which of necessity must be determined and administered by the Federation. The customs revenues, unlike those of Rhodesia, are shared with the regions.

[2] This point of view may reflect primarily the fact that the political party in power in Western Nigeria constitutes the Opposition in the Federal Parliament.

TABLE 8.2 TAX REVENUES BY LEVEL OF GOVERNMENT, NIGERIA, 1961–1962 BUDGET ESTIMATES IN MILLIONS OF POUNDS

Collected by	West-ern Nigeria	North-ern Nigeria	East-ern Nigeria	Total Regions	Fed-eral	Total
Federal:						
Company Tax					4.6	4.6
Customs and Excise:						
Tobacco	2.7	1.9	1.9	6.5		6.5
Motor Fuel	2.3	1.9	1.6	5.8		5.8
Distributable Pool	3.5	5.6	4.1	13.2	33.6	46.8
Export Taxes	6.6	4.4	2.1	13.1		13.1
Mining Royalties	0.9	0.6	1.0	2.5	1.6	4.1
Miscellaneous	—	—	—	—	3.9	3.9
Total	16.0	14.4	10.7	41.1	43.7	84.8
*Regions:**						
Personal Income Tax	1.0	0.5	3.5	5.0	2.4	7.4
Personal Tax		1.3		1.3		1.3
Produce Sales Taxes	0.8	0.7	0.8	2.3		2.3
Motor Fuel Taxes			0.3	0.3		0.3
License Taxes	0.7	0.7	0.6	2.0	0.8	2.8
Miscellaneous						
Total	2.5	3.2	5.2	10.9	3.2	14.1
Total	18.5	17.6	15.9	52.0	46.9	98.9

* Including taxes collected by the Federation for Lagos only.

The only regional levies of any magnitude are the personal income taxes (plus the personal tax and the *jangali*, or cattle tax, in Northern Nigeria); the produce sales taxes, collected through the marketing boards; the motor vehicle and other licenses, which in general are kept uniform among the regions; an entertainment tax, which produces little revenue; and in the East, a motor fuel tax. The regions are permitted to impose motor fuel levies in addition to the Federal customs and excises, but only Eastern Nigeria does so. The regional personal income taxes are by no means uniform, differing in rates and, particularly, in the personal allowance systems.

Prevailing Attitudes

The attitude of the regional governments on the question of taxes is that of states in most federal systems: they argue that they have inadequate revenue sources compared to their functions. This feeling is particularly strong in the West—again, perhaps, reflecting political differences. The heavy reliance on customs, excises, and export duties, with revenue subject to frequent change as economic conditions vary and with rates set by the Federal government, makes regional budgeting dffiicult. There is little elasticity in the regional budgets, with no place to turn in a fiscal emergency except to the Federal government.

The general argument is made that the Federal government has relatively far too much money at its disposal, while the regions have not nearly enough, with consequent unbalance in relative expenditures on the respective functions of the various levels of government. Given the over-all revenue structure, about the only significant avenue of reform is to increase the size of the distributable pool, so as to assign more federally collected revenue to the regions.

From a longer-range standpoint, certain other problems confront the regions. As domestic manufacturing increases, a smaller percentage of basic produce is exported, and thus export duties fall. As individual enterprises grow and become companies, the revenue goes to the Federal government instead of the regions. On the other hand, as income rises the personal income tax will be increasingly productive of revenue. Typically, as countries have developed economically, the income tax has grown in importance relative to the indirect taxes, and this trend almost certainly will occur in Nigeria. At the same time, taxes on property, which fall within the scope of the regions and their local governments, can be expanded over time and can lessen the reliance of the regions on sums allocated by the Federal government.

EAST AFRICA

The three mainland East African countries—Uganda, Kenya, and Tanganyika—while not comprising a federation in the usual sense of that term, have certain elements of federalism, and a very high degree of uniformity and common administration of their tax systems. The cooperation among them provides a significant illustration of how coordination can be attained among countries that are not technically federated.

The Countries

A brief word on the three countries is desirable as an introduction. In regard to population, Tanganyika, with 9 million people, is the largest, Kenya and Uganda each having about 6.5 million inhabitants. Uganda, one of the last sections of Africa to come under European domination, became a British protectorate in 1894, and gained its independence in October, 1962. It has certain federal elements in its own governmental structure, which will be described later in the chapter. There are relatively few Europeans in Uganda.

Most of the merchants and a few plantation owners are Indian, but primarily Uganda is a purely African country; coffee is the major crop, and most people live on their individual farms rather than in towns or villages.

Kenya, on the other hand, has a large number of Europeans; the white highlands are farmed by Europeans who settled in the country shortly after 1900, and Nairobi is basically a European-Indian city. Much of Kenya outside the coastal strip was wilderness, largely uninhabited, when the British made Uganda a protectorate, and control of the country was taken by the British largely to protect the rail route to Uganda and to keep the Germans out. The white settlers of Kenya long sought self-governing status but never received it; after substantial violence during the Mau Mau uprising of the early fifties, peace was gradually restored, and a constitution agreed upon early in 1962, so that the country will become independent on December 12, 1963.

Tanganyika is by far the largest of the three in area, with a widely scattered population, much desert country, an inadequate transportation system, and low per capita income. Taken over by the Germans in the 1890's, it passed into British trusteeship after World War I, and was granted independence in 1961.

A fourth East African country, one which participates in some of the common services, is Zanzibar, with a population of only 300,000. Zanzibar, long ruled by a Sultan whose ancestors moved from Oman, became a British protectorate in 1891. Independence, delayed by the inability of the Arab and African groups to agree on a constitution, will become effective December 10, 1963.

Development of Tax Coordination

The idea of cooperation among the territories dates back to the period immediately after World War I. But the path to closer ties was a slow and rugged one, largely because of the fear of the Africans in Uganda and Tanganyika of a "white" Kenya dominating the entire area. Some cooperation developed in the thirties, and this was replaced in the forties by a more formal organization, with the establishment in 1947 of the East Africa High Commission (now East Africa Common Services Organization) and a Central Legislative Assembly. So far as taxation is concerned, it was originally intended that the Central Legislative Assembly should have the power to set customs and excise tax rates, but this plan was abandoned.

Coordination of the tax structures and administration of the three territories had actually begun long before a formal organization was set up. In 1917, internal free trade and a common customs system were established by Kenya and Uganda, and joint administration was established. The Tanganyika tariff was merged with the others in a series of steps, and the customs department joined in 1949. The administration of customs and excise became a High Commission service in 1948. Subsequently, in 1952, the Central Legislative Assembly enacted a Customs Management Act and an Excise Tax Management Act. The rates of duties, however, are technically set by the legislatures of each territory. Income taxation was first introduced in Kenya; when the other two countries levied it in 1940, uniformity and joint administration were established. The power over the income tax structure was ultimately given to the Central Legislative Assembly, which enacted an Income Tax Management Act in 1952 (replaced by a new act in 1958). Thus the income tax structures are of necessity uniform, but the rates and personal allowances are set by the territorial legislatures, and may vary.

Despite the fact that the power to set customs and excise and income tax rates rests with the territorial legislatures, a very high degree of uniformity is attained. Tariff changes are discussed and agreed upon in advance by a committee made up of the Permanent Secretaries of Finance and Commerce and Industry of the three countries, with technical advice from the Commissioner of Customs. The changes are then enacted by the legislatures. There have been only a very few cases in which agreement has been impossible, with consequent slight differences in the tariffs. There are no tariff barriers within the territory covered by the three countries. The allocation of customs and excise revenue is made on the basis of the destination of the goods. When goods are imported for use in a particular territory and used in that territory, no complications arise. When, however, subsequent transshipment to another territory occurs, the shipper is required to fill out a transfer form indicating the territory of final destination. No additional duty is payable.

In the income tax field, likewise, despite the setting of rates by the territories, almost complete uniformity is attained. Although the rates have at times varied slightly, they are now entirely uniform. There are minor differences in personal allowances in Zanzibar, which is a party to the common income tax but not customs duties, and Kenya provides an additional allowance for old people that the others do not. Income tax rate changes are discussed in advance by the finance ministers of the three territories and announced in the budget messages at the same time. The Income Tax Management Act provides a very detailed statement of the income tax structure (apart from tax rates and personal allowances), dealing with the concept of income, the treatment of special forms of income, deductions, tax returns, assessments, appeals, collection, depreciation, and allocation of income by territory. Thus, in fact, a much greater coordination of personal income tax is found than in Nigeria, despite the fact that the latter is a single country and East Africa is not.

The Revenue Situation

As shown in Table 8.3, the great bulk of the revenues of the three territories comes from the common taxes. Thus 76% of Uganda's tax revenue, 88% of Tanganyika's, and 85% of Kenya's are col-

TABLE 8.3 EAST AFRICAN TERRITORIAL REVENUE, 1961–1962
BUDGET ESTIMATES IN THOUSANDS OF POUNDS

Revenue	Uganda	Tanganyika	Kenya	Total
Common Administration:				
Income Tax	3,300	4,100	10,000	
Customs Duties	6,350	8,176	9,100	
Excise Taxes	2,770	2,474	3,200	
Total	12,420	14,750	22,300	49,470
Separate Administration:				
Personal Tax	628*	950	1,700	
Export Duties	2,440	45	0	
License, Stamp, and				
Miscellaneous	891	955	2,352	
Total	3,959	1,950	4,052	9,961
Total	16,379	16,700	26,352	59,431

* Expired in 1962.

lected by the joint administration. The major taxes operated individually by the countries are the personal taxes, license taxes (primarily on motor vehicles), and, in Uganda, export taxes.

Merits and Difficulties

The East African system has worked very well in many respects. The uniform tariff, with no duties for shipments among the three countries, has provided a common market of more than 23 million people, one of the largest in Africa, and has, without question, stimulated the economic development of the area, particularly of industry, and is likely to do so even more in the future. The lack of internal tariffs and the joint customs administration have materially reduced manpower needs and expenses of collection. Also, a single uniform income tax structure has greatly simplified the task of administration, allowed more specialization in administrative personnel, aided taxpayer compliance, and facilitated economic development of the region as a whole. And, at least theoretically, the autonomy of the three territories over tax rates and allowances has been maintained.

On the other hand, the system has given rise to certain difficulties, which were responsible for the appointment of the Raisman Commission, whose report was made in 1961. These can be summarized briefly:

1. The most widespread discontent has been over tariff policy. Kenya, which has been in the best position to develop industry, has sought extensive protection, which the other two territories opposed, since, as a consequence of higher duties, they had to pay higher prices for goods consumed. To aggravate the problem, as protected Kenya industry developed, the other territories lost their customs revenue, while Kenya gained the income tax revenue from the new enterprises. Furthermore, the Kenya marketing boards would often sell Kenya goods on the foreign market more cheaply than in Uganda and Tanganyika, where the tariff protected the boards from foreign competition. Kenya and, to a limited extent, the others have at times interfered with the completely free flow of farm products by marketing board controls.

2. There have been some complaints about the operation of the customs system. When goods are imported into Kenya, and then subsequently transferred to one of the other countries, Kenya receives the customs revenue unless a transfer form is supplied. With shipments by rail, air, or post, there is no leakage, because the form must be filed before the shipment will be accepted by the carrier. But with motor transport, there is no such assurance. Concern over the question by Uganda led to systematic road checks, which indicated that the leakage was not of significant volume.

The other operational question is that of the appropriate value figure to use on goods no longer identifiable in reference to the original import because of processing, breaking bulk, etc. In practice, a 0.7 factor is used to reduce the figure to the imported price. While this is an arbitrary approach, it has produced relatively good results.

3. The income tax operation gave rise to two major complaints, both of which have, in part at least, been remedied as a result of recommendations of the Raisman Commission. One related to the allocation of individual income earned in one territory by the residents of another. The original formula assigned one half of such income to each of the two territories; this has been changed to give it all to the territory of origin.

The second complaint was a long-standing charge that Kenya received a disproportionate share of company tax because no reference was made in the formula to the sales made from Kenya into the other territories, when there was no actual place of business in the destination territories. The solution to this problem was the distributable pool approach, noted below. There have also been complaints about the allocation of tax on incomes of Common Services Organization employees, a high percentage of whom live in Kenya.

4. A more fundamental difficulty has been the inflexibility of the revenues of each of the territories. So long as the territories accept the principle that customs, excises, and income taxes must be uniform or nearly so, no government can vary its revenue from these sources without agreement of the others, and this is not always forthcoming. As noted, the revenues other than the common ones are of minor significance. This problem has been less serious than it might have been, because the revenue needs of the three territories have not differed fundamentally from the yield of the taxes at the agreed-upon rates. However, particularly Uganda and Tanganyika are somewhat concerned about the general inflexibility and potential inadequacy.

5. The methods of determining income tax and customs duty rates have been subjected to some criticism. It is maintained that frequently decisions are made largely on the basis of horse trading and the strength of personality and bargaining skill of the representatives of particular countries. Yet on the whole the decisions have been made without serious conflict.

6. Finally, in somewhat broader terms, there exists a fundamental deficiency, relative to the usual federal structure. Normally, when several territories are willing to accept common customs and taxes despite substantial variations in per capita income and economic growth, they do so in part because the common taxes are accompanied by grants or expenditure programs which transfer money from the richer to the poorer areas of the federal system. But in East Africa, with no central government in the true sense of that term, there has been no system for transfers by grants. This deficiency led the Raisman Commission to recommend the distributable pool system described below.

Solutions to the Problems

Apart from minor adjustments to improve the system made from time to time, a major change was made in 1961, following the recommendations of the Raisman Commission.

138

So far as taxation is concerned, the major recommendation of the Raisman Commission was the establishment of a distributable pool, a recommendation which the territories accepted, although, in the case of Tanganyika, for a two-year period only. The primary aims were to provide some redistribution of revenue from Kenya, which gains greater benefits from the common market than the others, to the other two territories, as well as to lessen the complaints that Kenya receives an unfairly large sum of company tax revenue. Specifically, there is allocated to the pool 40% of the revenues of customs and excise duties. One half of the revenue is used to finance various services of the Common Services Organization, and the other half is distributed in equal shares to the three territories. Costs of administration of the taxes were made a first charge against the revenues. While Tanganyika felt that the change did not go far enough, there was general agreement that this represented a step in the right direction.

As the three countries gain their independence, there has been speculation about more drastic changes. There had been some fear that the whole joint-services operation might break up, with elimination of the common market and establishment of separate customs and tax administrations. Such a change was opposed by the World Bank report on Tanganyika and the Raisman Commission; the three governments appear today to accept the position that the advantages of the common market and common administration are such that they should be retained. It is a question in which African politicians have shown little interest; whether the new governments can coordinate their efforts as well in attaining mutually acceptable conclusions remains to be seen. But the three countries, while not without rivalries, have many common interests, and with Kenya an "African" instead of a "white" country, there are no significant traditional hostilities, and continued cooperation should be a very real possibility.

The other possibility is that of the move toward actual federation on the Nigerian pattern, a move originally sponsored by Tanganyika's President Nyerere. Initially, the plan found little support in Uganda, largely because of the fear that the federation would be dominated by a "white" Kenya. With this fear eliminated, there is less opposition in Uganda, but some fear on the part of Buganda that, while it can probably control Uganda, it could not control the entire federation. In 1963 there has been increased support for the move toward federation.

The Uganda and Kenya Internal Problem

The establishment of a constitution in Uganda was delayed by the demands of Buganda, by far the largest and wealthiest unit of the country, for a high degree of autonomy. Actually, there was substantial support in Buganda for separate independence. Thus it was necessary to grant Buganda essentially the position of a state in a federal system; agreement on this point was reached in 1961, but without agreement on financial aspects. In part, to aid in a solution to this problem, a Fiscal Commission was appointed by the Uganda government in 1962, which rendered its report in May of that year. In its memorandum to the Fiscal Commission, the Buganda government argued that it had rights to all taxation arising out of the land of the Kingdom, activities connected with the use of the land, and the people residing on it—thus to all personal and income taxation, land taxes, export duties, and excise duties on goods produced in Buganda. There would be left to Uganda only the customs duties and company taxation. On the other hand, existing grants by Uganda to Buganda would cease. The Fiscal Commission was unwilling to accept this request and suggested only minor increases in the taxing powers of Buganda.

Attention has also been given in Kenya in the last two years to the question of allocation of functions and tax revenue among the central, regional, and local governments. A Fiscal Commission studied the issues and made recommendations.

CONCLUDING OBSERVATIONS

In these three instances of federal finance, great stress was placed on the development or reform of the tax systems, upon the need for uniformity of customs duties, excises, and income taxes, as well as upon unified administration. Several factors played a part in this emphasis. One was the urgent need for maximum efficiency in administration of the taxes, given the general shortage of personnel in these countries. A second factor was the desire to minimize nuisance for the taxpayer in the form of duplicating returns and varying rules for calculation of income. A third was the strong desire to avoid discriminatory double taxation by more than one territory. Finally, great attention was paid, in the interests of economic development, to the need to ensure the internal free flow of trade and avoidance of tax differentials—particularly of company taxes.

On the other hand, some attention was paid to the need for the fiscal autonomy of the territories and the desire to ensure them some independent revenues and some influence in the setting of the tax rates. In addition, in the allocation of the yield of various taxes, recognition was given to the total expenditure needs of the territories. However, while the autonomy argument was stressed, it actually played a very subordinate role to that of efficiency and uniformity.

As a consequence, a high percentage of all tax revenue is collected by the central administration: in Rhodesia, 76% of the territorial revenues and 89% of the tax revenue of all governments; in Nigeria 79% of the regional government revenues and 86% of the tax revenues of all governments; and in East Africa 83% of the territorial revenues. With a portion of this revenue the rates are technically subject to control of the territories, but in fact this power is effective in only a few instances—the motor fuel taxes in Rhodesia, for example. While the territories can vary their surcharges on income tax in Rhodesia, in fact they do not, with one exception.

More specifically, the tax systems which have developed have the following major characteristics:

1. In all three instances there is a single uniform customs and excise system with common administration and uniform rates (with minor rate exceptions in East Africa), and complete free trade within the federations. The rates are set by the central government in Nigeria and Rhodesia, and technically by the territories in East Africa. In all instances the basic structure (apart from rates) is established by the central legislative body.

2. All three have uniform, centrally administered company income taxes; uniformity in this field is regarded as essential for economic development and effective enforcement.

3. In the personal income tax field, common structural legislation (excluding rates and personal allowances) is found in all three areas. In Rhodesia, the rates are set by the Federation except for the territorial surcharges. In East Africa, the rates and allowances, while technically set by each territory, are in fact uniform (with minor exceptions). Only in Nigeria do the rates and allowances differ, and each region has its own administration.

4. The territorial governments are confined, except for Nigeria, to relatively minor taxes, the most important of which are the graduated personal taxes, export duties (Nigeria and Uganda only, centrally administered in the former), motor vehicle and other licenses, produce sales taxes (Nigeria), and, for the cities, property rates.

Since the revenues from the taxes left to the territories are grossly inadequate, a portion of the centrally collected taxes is returned to the territories. There are two basic rules of distribution:

1. The "origin" rule—that is, allocation on the basis of where

the activity that gave rise to the tax took place—is used in several instances:

  a. Export duties—Nigeria.
  b. Motor fuel taxes—Nigeria, Rhodesia.
  c. Customs and excise (less 6%)—East Africa.
  d. Personal and company income taxes (except 40% of the proceeds of the latter from manufacturing and financial firms, in East Africa).
  e. The territorial surcharge on income tax—Rhodesia.
  f. Tobacco duties and excises—Nigeria.
  g. A portion of mining royalties—Nigeria.

2. The distributable pool, whereby revenues are allocated on the basis of a formula indicating need, is used to some extent in all three jurisdictions:

  a. Income tax, Rhodesia, on the basis of preset percentages derived from comparison of expenditure needs and other revenues.
  b. A total of 40% of the company tax revenues from manufacturing and financial establishments, and 6% of customs duty, East Africa. Half of the pool funds is used to finance the Common Services Organization expenditure; the other half is divided among the territories in equal shares.
  c. In Nigeria, a portion of import duties and mining rents and royalties.

The emphasis on central government control and administration has, on the whole, resulted in a high degree of efficiency of operation, and minimization of double taxation, multiplicity of returns, and other nuisances. But at the same time it has produced the inevitable complaint of lack of flexibility and real financial autonomy on the part of the territories, and frequently a general complaint of inadequate territorial funds relative to expenditure needs. Some of the intended fiscal autonomy has proved nominal; all three territories in Rhodesia have found it necessary to use the maximum figure of the permitted surcharges on income (with one exception). The East African countries have considered uniformity of duties and income taxes to be imperative. The revenue inadequacies have led to demands for greater allocations, particularly of customs duties, into the distributable pools.

Thus, the experience of these new federations suggests that it is, in fact, possible to avoid many of the major evils of tax aspects of federalism found in older countries. But to do so requires a degree of centralization of taxation which reduces the fiscal autonomy of the subordinate units beyond the levels regarded as tolerable in the older federations. The optimum balance between uniformity and efficiency, on the one hand, and territorial fiscal autonomy, on the other, cannot be defined in any scientific way, but it is obvious that the optimum is not likely to be the same under all conditions. Newly developing economies must of necessity rely heavily on customs duties, which must be federally administered; thus, almost of necessity the optimum balance in new federations requires more centralization than in old. The urgency of economic development may make uniformity of income taxation more important than it is in established economies. But in the older, long-established federations, the division of taxing powers was often made with little thought of uniformity and efficiency considerations, and some readjustment toward greater centralization might well be justified. But once various taxing powers are strongly implanted in the subordinate units, considerations of prestige and "states' rights" may make readjustment very difficult. The new federations may well move gradually away from such great centralization as they now have—but this move may be considerably less difficult than the reverse moves with the countries that started their federal existence centuries ago with complete emphasis on the need for fiscal autonomy, and complete neglect of economic considerations.

SELECTED REFERENCES

Hicks, U. K., *et al.*, *Federalism and Economic Growth in Underdeveloped Countries*. London: George Allen and Unwin, 1961.

Rhodesia
Draft Federal Scheme—Report of the Fiscal Commission. London: H.M.S.O., 1952.
Report of the Advisory Commission on the Review of the Constitution of Rhodesia and Nyasaland. London: H.M.S.O., 1960.
Phoenix Group, *Planning the Development of the Wealth of Three Nations*. Salisbury: 1960.

Nigeria
Nigeria: Report of the Fiscal Commission. London: H.M.S.O., 1958.

East Africa
East Africa: Report of the Economic and Fiscal Commission. London: H.M.S.O., 1961.
Report of the Uganda Fiscal Commission. Entebbe: Government Printer, 1962.
Government of Kenya, *Report of the Fiscal Commission*. Nairobi: Government Printer, 1963.

9 Tax Policy and Economic Development

T HE PRIMARY ECONOMIC GOAL of the underdeveloped countries of the world, and particularly the newly independent or about-to-become independent countries of Africa, is a substantial increase in the rate of economic growth, which, it is hoped, will bring the countries in a relatively short period to the levels of per capita real income comparable to those of the more developed economies. Attainment of this goal, in turn, requires two major accomplishments:

1. Provision of additional basic governmental services, particularly in education, public health, and transport, which are imperative for the growth of the remainder of the economy.

2. A higher rate of capital formation in production facilities, whether undertaken in the governmental or private sectors. The specific goal is, of course, not the highest possible rate of capital formation, but the lowest rate that will permit the maximum rate of growth in GNP regarded as feasible under the circumstances.

The first requires transfer of resources to the governmental sector of the economy for the production of the services. The second requires transfer of resources to capital formation, either strictly in the private sector, or in or through the governmental sector. There are four major sources from which the resources may come:

1. Outside the country.

2. Present use for consumption.

3. Present use in production of capital goods of a type regarded as not contributing to economic growth, as, for example, too many office buildings.

4. Idle or partially idle resources, primarily manpower.

Under usual circumstances, the second source would appear to offer the maximum potentialities. The fourth one in itself offers little opportunity for growth, since better utilization of manpower usually requires considerable investment in capital. The first alternative is limited by the willingness and ability of a government to obtain foreign loans; the third is not usually very significant, although some countries have had considerable overbuilding of office space.

The key to economic growth is, of course, the transfer and better utilization of resources, not merely a shift of money. Nevertheless, financial transfers will, within the framework of the market economy, facilitate the transfer of real resources. Transfers to government from individuals who would spend the funds on consumption or invest them in outlets of limited significance for growth make it possible to obtain the factors for governmental services or capital formation without resorting to borrowing or money creation, both of which would result in competition of governmental and private spending for the resources. It is true that if the funds would have merely become idle or have been sent outside the country, the government could have created an equivalent amount of purchasing power and obtained the resources without inflation. But such action is often difficult in the framework of monetary and banking institutions in underdeveloped countries, and estimates of the amounts may be wrong. Likewise, to the extent to which resources are idle for other reasons, they can be obtained by the government through money creation instead of transfer of funds, and such a policy may be regarded as entirely justifiable. However, when the initial recipients spend the money, the total level of spending may exceed the total level of output, and the government must absorb funds to prevent inflation. To the extent to which private savings and capital formation can be increased without government participation, no transfer of funds to government is necessary.

The primary instrument for the transfer of funds to the government to facilitate transfer of resources is taxation. This method theoretically, at least, may also be used to provide incentive to increase private savings and the private-sector rate of capital formation, although, as will be seen, there is greater likelihood of the opposite effect. More specifically, in a developing economy, the tax system may be used to accomplish the following functions:

1. Curtailing consumption and thus freeing resources for governmental services or capital formation.

2. Reallocating resources from investments regarded as having little beneficial effect upon economic development (e.g., office buildings) to those of greater benefit for growth.

3. Providing a flow of funds into government hands to facilitate the transfer of resources.

4. Providing incentive to alter economic behavior in such a way as to facilitate economic growth, such as providing added incentive to save, to enter the market sector, to work longer periods, to undertake private-sector capital formation.

The first and third functions are the same as in mature economies; the second is not usually regarded as significant in such economies; the fourth may or may not be desired in mature economies, depending on the relationship between planned savings and investment opportunities at full employment and other considerations. However, while the first function may be the same in all economies, the task of performing it is far more difficult in an underdeveloped economy because the margin between actual consumption and bare subsistence is very slight.

Regardless of the nature of the economy, there is ever-present danger that the tax system, while directly accomplishing the prime goals, may, because of its compulsory nature, have serious adverse effects upon the functioning of the economy and thus reduce national income below potential levels. This danger is particularly great in an economy with a very limited margin over subsistence and a high percentage of the population still primarily engaged in subsistence agriculture rather than in producing for market. The primary dangers are those of restricting instead of increasing the incentives to work, to participate in the market economy, to save, and to develop and expand businesses. There is particular danger that persons will find it advantageous to withdraw into the subsistence economy instead of participating more fully in the market economy.

Thus, the framing of the tax structure must give particular attention to the minimization of adverse incentive effects and maximization of incentive reactions which further the attainment of the goal. The extent to which these objectives can be attained will, in turn, constitute an important element in the determination of the optimum rate of economic growth, which cannot be defined without regard to the tax-incentive factors. Unfortunately, two major dilemmas are encountered. In the first place, as will be discussed later, the type of tax that most successfully recovers for the government a portion of the gains of the rising national income is the type that is most likely to interfere with incentives. Second, the general tax environment of an underdeveloped economy is unsuited to a high degree of perfection of the tax structure. Various significant features of such an economy include low levels of literacy and record keeping; inadequate numbers of trained tax administrators and auditors; unsatisfactory land title situations; limited use of bank accounts; and the importance of the subsistence segment of the economy, the output of which is difficult to ascertain and value.

The remainder of this chapter will be devoted to the question of how the tax systems of developing economies can most satisfactorily be adjusted to attain the goals outlined, drawing upon the experience of the eight countries of the study.

INCOME TAXATION

In mature economies, the income tax is widely accepted as the most suitable primary source of revenue. The applicability of this rule to underdeveloped economies requires careful consideration. Even in such economies, however, income taxation offers several primary advantages. In many respects the income tax is the most effective way to reach the above-subsistence income of those groups which have attained such levels, the tax being adjusted in terms of the amount of such excess and made progressive relative to it, if desired. No other taxes can be adjusted in such a precise fashion. A large portion of the tax, under such conditions as those prevailing in tropical Africa, will be obtained from civil servants, business executives, employees, and professional men. Taxation of these persons will likely have few harmful effects on economic development since they are not engaged in undertaking significant business investment. The tax will recover a portion of the gains made from economic growth and particularly will catch the "unearned income"—speculative gains, increases in land values, etc.—taxation of which presumably has little effect on economic growth. The direct burden of the tax makes persons cognizant of their responsibilities toward government. The yield is more stable than that of the major alternative sources. Finally, the tax conforms with widely accepted standards of equity. It can be used to bring about a redistribution of income—but this is much less significant under conditions such as those of tropical Africa than in other underdeveloped areas because of the absence of large private fortunes and incomes.

However, income taxation under such conditions suffers from rather obvious limitations which, of necessity, restrict the relative reliance on it compared to the use in more developed economies. The first problem is administrative. Underdeveloped countries all suffer from a severe shortage of trained personnel for administrative work of all kinds, including income tax audit. To the extent to which this very scarce personnel is used for income tax administration, it is not available for other purposes. Other than in the top income and wage earner groups, standards of literacy and record keeping are such that accurate determination of income is virtually impossible. Application of the tax to subsistence farming income is particularly difficult because of the problems of determining the amounts and values of this income.

Inevitably, a tax which takes a certain (and usually progressive) percentage of income presumably has some effect on economic incentives. If subject to income tax, a person on the margin between subsistence and market-economy production may be driven back to the subsistence economy entirely if his market-economy income is taxed. However, as with more developed economies, the effect may be the reverse; he may seek to work more in the market sector in order to maintain his given income from that sector. The net over-all effect is uncertain. In practice, administrative considerations dictate that persons on this margin are not subject to tax. Similarly, it is impossible to say whether there is significant net effect on the willingness of persons to save or to undertake the risk of business development; the greater the marginal rates, however, the greater is the risk of such effects. One disadvantage cannot be challenged: an income tax provides no incentive to save more and consume less, and a relatively high percentage of tax is borne by those persons who presumably save relatively high percentages of their incomes. The tax must, therefore, be absorbed in part out of savings that would have been used for economic development. There may be no net loss from the government's absorption of this sum, but there is, at the same time, no gain so far as total capital formation is concerned; the intent of the tax program relative to economic growth has not been fully accomplished.

Thus, while an income tax has merit as an element in the tax structure of a developing economy, and its yield will grow progressively as the economy expands, the revenue potentialities are somewhat limited. In its usual form, the tax must be confined to a relatively small percentage of the population, and the rates presumably must be kept lower than would be regarded as tolerable in a more developed economy. Also, given the problems of administrative personnel, even with the limited coverage of the taxes, a maximum degree of simplification consistent with equity must be maintained.

Review of the income taxes of the eight African countries indicates conformity with these observations in considerable measure. The personal allowances are such, from £200 up (except in Nigeria), as to exclude all but a relatively small number of higher-income families. Other than in Eastern and Western Nigeria, which are discussed below, less than 1% of the population of the countries is covered by the income taxes; the figures range from 0.2% in several countries to 0.9% in Rhodesia. There is substantially less constraint on the rates. While the initial rates are relatively low, by the income figure of £2,500, the rate is 25% or higher in all jurisdictions except one; by £5,000 it is 42% or higher in all except one. The maximum is 75% in the East African countries and two others. At the higher income levels the burdens are greater in most of the countries than in the United States, and greater in some than in in the United Kingdom. Only Ghana has substantially lower rates. There is little complaint, however, that rates of this magnitude are, in fact, seriously retarding development; on the other hand, very few persons are subject to the high rates.

In the matter of simplicity, the taxes have left much to be desired. They were initially modeled on the United Kingdom tax, applied primarily to Europeans, and administered by European staffs. As the economies have developed, more and more non-Europeans have become subject to tax, and the staffs have become progressively less adequate as expatriate personnel have left. The need for simplification of the taxes is now widely recognized. Ghana made drastic changes in 1961, eliminating all personal deductions and allowances except a standard consolidated allowance. The East African tax was simplified to some extent in 1961, and further changes are under consideration.

Despite the very limited coverage, the revenue yield is significant. Rhodesia and Kenya obtain 21% of their revenue from the personal income tax, and the other six countries (except Sierra Leone) obtain between 7% and 12%. On the whole, the African experience suggests that a fairly complicated income tax can be administered with a substantial degree of success in an underdeveloped country so long as adequate personnel trained in more developed economies are available and the tax is limited to a relatively small percentage of the population. As outside technical personnel are lost and reliance must be placed entirely on indigenous staff, the complications of the taxes have made administration difficult and have led to simplification. But the simplified taxes still preserve the principles of income taxation, with merely some reduction in refinements of equity. The over-all experience of these countries with income taxation is encouraging with regard to the use of the tax in under-developed economies, but it also shows the danger of superimposing taxes developed in mature economies onto less developed ones.

Apart from the question of the desirability of the use of income taxation is that of the best income tax structure. Again, particular features of such taxation that are regarded as most suitable in a developed economy may be completely unsatisfactory in an under-developed one. For example, failure to tax capital gains—as is the practice in the African countries following the British tradition—allows a type of income particularly suitable for taxation, under the circumstances, to go tax-free—namely, gains from speculation and from increases in land values. Allowing gains from increases in stock prices to be freed from tax may have some merit in terms of incentives relating to development, but freeing other gains has none whatsoever. The system of credits for dependents most suitable for a Western society may be completely unsuitable in others; with multiple wives and "extended families," the usual system breaks down. The first step taken in Africa was to limit the number of allowances for children to four and the number for wives to one, and to restrict severely the number of other eligible dependents. The rule on children sometimes is justified also on the grounds of the desire to hold down the birth rate—but the effect along these lines is doubtful. When Ghana revised its tax in 1961 and Northern Nigeria introduced a new levy in 1962, a single consolidated allowance, regardless of the number of dependents, was established. This violates usual standards of equity but may be the most workable alternative under the circumstances.

THE PERSONAL TAX APPROACH

While income taxation in the usual form may be unsuitable for the mass of the population of underdeveloped economies, there is the possibility of using a direct tax of broad application, in the form of what is known in Africa as the personal tax. As the tax operates in Uganda, Kenya, and elsewhere, all persons (or, typically, all adult males) are subject to a minimum tax, and those with higher incomes are assessed on a graduated scale, up to a maximum figure that is reached roughly at the level of income at which the income tax becomes effective. Assessment is usually made on a local basis, by a committee of county and village officials (in Uganda) or nonofficials who are familiar with local conditions. For employees, the tax is based on actual income; for the typical semisubsistence farmer, it is based on external criteria of probable income such as acreage and number of cows. Non-Africans are usually assessed at the maximum unless they file a return to demonstrate lower income.

In Eastern and Western Nigeria, the personal taxes are included in the income tax structure, the latter extended by a minimum tax rule down to the lowest income groups. The portions of the taxes applying to the lower income levels are, however, administered in much the same fashion as the personal taxes of other jurisdictions.

On the whole, the operation of these personal taxes appears to be satisfactory, and the experience confirms the possibility of using mass direct taxes in underdeveloped economies. While only rough equity is attained in assessment, the results appear to be reasonably good, and enforcement standards are usually high; certainly there is no mass escape, as evidenced by the numbers of taxpayers relative to the total population. Administration is largely in African hands. The principle of direct taxation is firmly established, reliance on indirect taxes is reduced, and, in time, the taxes can be perfected so far as equity is concerned. These taxes have two potentially beneficial economic effects. Since the taxes must be paid in money, they force the subsistence farmers to sell produce or labor services. The graduation does not become effective for the great mass of the farmers at the subsistence margin; for those who are affected, there is less danger that the tax will drive them back to greater emphasis on subsistence farming. Secondly, so long as a person remains in the same tax bracket, he has incentive to earn more, not less, since the additional income gives rise to no added tax liability.

There is some danger at the bracket points, where the marginal rate often exceeds 100% as the person moves into a higher bracket, and thus he may be discouraged from gaining added income. But once he is in the bracket, he again has incentive to earn more, not less. Furthermore, to the extent to which assessments are based on potential rather than actual income, incentive is given to work harder. This rule, however, may violate usual standards of equity.

A variant of the personal tax in Northern Nigeria is the *jangali*, applied to the Fulani herdsmen in lieu of personal tax, based on the number of cows, and designed in large measure to force the sale of a portion of the herd. The goal of the Fulani is typically to maximize the size of the herd rather than to gain money income from the sale of the produce, to the detriment of development of the economy.

CORPORATE TAXATION

In an underdeveloped economy the tax potential from corporations usually exceeds that from individuals at typical rates. In the eight African countries, the company tax yield exceeds the yield of the personal income tax in all jurisdictions except Kenya and Zanzibar. In such economies a substantial portion of potentially taxable income is earned by a relatively small number of companies, often foreign-owned, and failure to tax their net income would allow a large portion of the potential tax base to escape. However, it is of course obvious that heavy corporate taxation can interfere with economic growth, both by taking funds which would be used for expansion and by lessening the incentives to expand. The magnitude of the adverse effect cannot be defined, but the dangers are such as to require caution in the use of the taxes. There is, however, the possibility that appropriate adjustments in company taxation may be helpful in attaining better use of resources in economic development.

First, because of these considerations, there is justification for holding the tax rates below those tolerable in the more developed economies. This has been the practice in the eight African countries, although the rates, in the range of $37\frac{1}{2}\%$ to 45%, are not far below those of the mature economies.

Second, so far as domestically held companies are concerned, there is merit in avoiding double taxation of dividend income—much more merit than in a highly developed economy. The African countries in the past provided complete credit at the dividend level for tax paid at the company level; all continue to do so on their basic company taxes except Ghana, while the East African countries now levy a supplementary 10% corporate tax for which no credit is allowed.

Third, special tax concessions to new or expanding industry may greatly reduce the potential adverse effect of the taxes upon company expansion, and also upon the expansion of smaller noncorporate businesses, to which the same rules usually apply. These concessions take two forms: general provisions applicable to all firms; and those granted only to specific firms upon request, under what is generally known as pioneer companies legislation.

One major general concession is the establishment of very liberal provisions for loss carry-forward, so that new firms or expanding firms that suffer losses in the first few years of operation will obtain subsequent tax reductions. Nigeria, Rhodesia, and the East African countries all permit unlimited carry-forward of losses; the period is limited to six years in Sierra Leone and 15 years in Ghana. A great advantage of this approach is that the risk of developing new enterprises is materially reduced, yet the actual relief is confined to the firms that need it, and the amount of the relief is dependent on actual losses and thus on need.

A second type of general concession is that which allows accelerated depreciation or, in other words, a very rapid write-off of new capital equipment in the early years of investment. This is particularly important for expansion of existing profitable businesses; the risk from the expansion is reduced, a tax-free loan in the form of deferment of taxes is provided, and so long as the company continues to expand, there is a net tax saving. The programs take two forms: initial allowances, in which the additional allowance in the first year reduces those in subsequent years, and the investment allowance, in which the additional amount in the first year does not reduce subsequent allowances. While the usefulness of such allowances in mature economies is open to serious question, in developing economies they offer significant potentialities without the administrative problems created by tax holidays, as noted below. The initial allowances encourage long-term capital investments more than other approaches, although in so doing they give particular advantages to capital-intensive techniques, which may be regarded as undesirable in labor-surplus economies. All eight of the African countries provide some form of allowance, usually of the initial variety, and Rhodesia and East Africa grant investment allowances. In Rhodesia the first-year combined initial and investment allowance on industrial equipment is 38%.

In reverse, if the government wishes to check investment along certain lines, it can deny the use of the special allowances in these fields, and even the deductibility of any depreciation charges. This policy has been followed to some extent in the African countries by adjusting the rates of the allowances according to the relative importance attached to the particular category of investment.

The pioneer-companies or tax-holiday type of legislation authorizes complete exemption from tax for a period of years, usually five, for new firms upon specific request and approval. In Africa the practice is confined to the three West African countries and is regarded as objectionable in East Africa and Rhodesia. The usual procedure is for the firm to file an application; this is reviewed by the Ministry of Trade and Commerce, in consultation with the Ministry of Finance, to ascertain the potential contribution of the firm to economic development. If this contribution is found to be significant, the application is approved. In both Ghana and Nigeria the *industry* must be approved as a pioneer industry before the applications of particular *firms* in the industry receive approval. The exemption is granted in Nigeria only if the total investment exceeds a certain figure, and the period of the exemption, between three and five years, depends on the amount of investment. Ghana used the program extensively in the middle and late fifties,[1] but

[1] See A. H. Smith, "Tax Relief for New Industries in Ghana," *National Tax Journal*, Vol. XI (December, 1958), pp. 362–370.

somewhat less in recent years, as the government has been inclined to the position that most industrial development must come through the government. In Nigeria, approval has been provided for about fifty industries between 1959 and 1962, and an approximately similar number were pending in 1962. The exemption covers all income taxation as well as dividends paid from earnings and allows complete carry-forward into subsequent periods of depreciation allowances on capital equipment.

The experience of these countries indicates clearly the difficulties of this approach for encouraging economic development. The greatest difficulty in Ghana and Nigeria has been the long delay in processing applications, often from five months to a year.[2] This delay not only is costly to the firms, but may actually result in investment taking place later than it would without the program, as firms which would have undertaken the investments anyway await approval of their applications. More speedy handling would require additional personnel, and they are very scarce under the circumstances.

A related difficulty is that of establishing clear-cut criteria for decision on the applications; neither Ghana nor Nigeria has solved this problem. Nominally, priority has been given to firms using primarily domestic materials and personnel, to those with large numbers of workers, and to those which appear to make a major contribution to economic development, in contrast, for example, to breweries or bottling plants. But the latter types are the ones which frequently make application and not infrequently are approved because of their indirect contribution to the development of a skilled labor force. Establishment and implementation of a completely logical set of criteria require a general level of planning and competency of staff which are out of the question in such economies. Furthermore, it is impossible to distinguish the projects which would be undertaken without the concession from those which would not be, and thus the net loss in revenue is much greater than necessary to obtain the new investment.

There are other difficulties as well. The gains to the firms from the concessions are sometimes offset by requirements as to location of plant and other factors imposed as conditions. There is also the question of renewals; if a firm insists that it must have an extension of the concession at the end of the five-year period, the government may be reluctant to deny it. There is danger of "hobo" enterprises— ones which require only short-term capital, and which liquidate at the end of the concession and move to a country that will grant the privilege for another period. There is also the basic issue relating

[2] See J. H. Perry, *Taxation and Economic Development in Ghana* (New York: United Nations, 1958), p. 44.

to monopoly. The concession is granted to one firm in an industry, and then a potential competitor seeks it; should this be granted?

Two international aspects should be noted. The effectiveness of the program for any one country is of course lessened as others in the area adopt the same program. Second, with foreign-held companies, some of the benefit of the tax saving may be lost in the form of higher taxes to the home country. There are means of avoiding this, however, and present British tax law allows the firm to retain the benefit from the concession.

There are also grave questions about the significance of the concessions for investment policy; at best, they represent merely one element in the picture. It is often argued that the advantage is mainly psychological; the concession is a symbol of favor toward private enterprise. But even this may be offset by other government policies, as it has been in large measure in Ghana.[3]

Thus the basic issue in the choice of the two methods is this: a program adjusted in light of the situation of the individual firm can, in theory, be most suitable in preventing the income tax structure from deterring investment, and in directing investment along the most desired lines. However, this approach gives rise to serious problems of implementation, problems difficult in any economy, and particularly in those in which competent administrative personnel are extremely scarce. This problem suggests that a general program of tax relief via loss carry-forward and accelerated depreciation is more suitable under the circumstances than pioneer companies legislation, with perhaps some adjustment by general rule of the rate of acceleration according to the estimated contribution of the general line of activity to the economic development program.

INCOME TAX CONCESSIONS ACCORDING TO USE OF FUNDS

One possible adjustment in income tax structures to minimize adverse effects of the tax upon savings is to permit deduction from taxable income of amounts used for certain types of financial investments. The difficulties lie partially in control; there is no entirely effective way of ensuring that the new investments are made from current income rather than merely from previous savings kept in other forms. Again, the marginal consideration applies; change in the tax law may have little effect in encouraging the

[3] See J. Heller and K. M. Kauffman, *Tax Incentives for Industry in Less Developed Countries* (Cambridge: Harvard Law School, 1963), for a detailed analysis of tax incentives.

investment but will cause substantial loss in revenue. Major equity questions may also be raised.

The final step in the direction of concessions is that of readjustment of the income tax into an expenditure tax along the Kaldor lines, as attempted on a very limited scale by India and Ceylon. The arguments are well known and need not be repeated. While the need to increase savings is greater in an underdeveloped country than in a mature one, the potential relative advantages of an expenditure tax over an income tax in accomplishing this would appear to be less, because of the importance of increased consumption as an incentive in such economies. Furthermore, the administration of an income tax is difficult enough in such countries if it is made to apply to any significant number of persons; the expenditure tax would add considerably to these administrative problems. The type of elaborate cross-checking system as proposed by Kaldor and Higgins, involving combinations of transactions, income, wealth, and expenditure taxes, while of potential merit in somewhat more developed economies, is clearly impossible for feasible operation in the African type of economic society.

INDIRECT TAXATION

In view of the potential conflict of income taxation with the incentives important for economic development, the desire to encourage savings at the expense of consumption, and the administrative problems of income taxation, it is widely argued that indirect taxation should play a major role in the tax structures of developing economies. In fact, of course, they typically do. In the eight African countries, customs and excises yield over 40% of the revenues in all of the countries except Rhodesia, and over 60% in five. From an economic standpoint, the primary argument for indirect taxes is that they are not directly related to the earning of income and thus, unlike income taxes, do not constitute a disincentive to earn monetary income. At the same time, since the indirect (commodity) taxes raise the costs of consumption relative to saving, incentive is provided to increase the percentage of income saved. By concentrating the burden upon persons spending high percentages of their incomes, these taxes force greater reduction in consumption per dollar of revenue than the income tax does, it is argued. If the taxes are imposed primarily upon luxury goods, not only can curtailment of luxury consumer spending be maximized, but reasonable accord with usual standards of equity can be attained. Basic subsistence expenditures can be freed of tax.

Furthermore, since the consumption taxes in developing economies apply primarily to imported goods, they can be used to curtail luxury spending on such goods and thus lessen foreign exchange difficulties which are often encountered with rapid growth, and free foreign exchange for industrial goods needed for economic development. Of the eight African countries, all concentrate the tariffs to a considerable degree on luxuries. In 1961, Ghana, which has experienced the greatest difficulty with balance of payments, adopted, on the advice of Kaldor, a supplement to the customs duties called the purchase tax, with rates as high as $66\frac{2}{3}\%$, in an effort to check luxury imports.

The final major argument for indirect taxes is the greater ease of administration, since the taxes can be collected from the importer or large producer. It is for this reason, more perhaps than any other, that colonial tax systems from the earliest days concentrated on customs duties, and movement away from them has been slow.

These arguments obviously have some merit. But there are conflicting considerations as well. The effectiveness of the taxes in reducing consumption is weakened to the extent to which savings are made to buy goods in the future, and it is expected that the tax will be permanent. While it is true that the indirect taxes do not directly impinge on income, they do affect the utility of the income. In countries moving from a very undeveloped state, from all indications, money income is desired by the mass of the population directly and immediately for the goods that can be obtained with it. Thus, to the extent to which these goods are taxed and made more expensive, the effect is the same as if the tax were imposed directly on income. Whether there will be a net increase or decrease in effort depends upon the relative importance of the income and substitution effects; but under such circumstances the net effect will differ little from that of an income tax. Duties on articles of widespread consumption may simply encourage persons to go back into the subsistence economy; very high taxes on luxury goods, such as the Ghana purchase tax, may shift purchases to other goods, materially impair incentives, and produce a hostile popular reaction. Certainly in Ghana and British Guiana, there were violent reactions to the sharp increases in taxes, to the detriment of political stability and economic growth.

Closely related are equity matters relating to the selection of commodities to be taxed. If a limited number of luxury goods are subjected to high rates, discrimination against the persons preferring these goods over substitutes is inevitable. If significant revenue is to be obtained, items of wider consumption are required, and equity considerations again arise. The tax must of necessity be collected at the time of importation or basic manufacture, and pyramiding of the tax burden plus unequal burden on various lines of consumption because of varying distribution margins are inevitable. With customs duties, the task of constructing tariffs that accomplish the desired ends is difficult. Moreover, high rates will encourage smuggling, already a problem of some magnitude in Nigeria and other countries. It is likewise difficult to keep producers' goods free of customs duties unless they are highly selective, and the cost of investment is artificially increased. A basic difficulty is created by the "catchall" categories in the tariffs. If there is none, as in Zanzibar, any item not falling within a defined category is duty-free, and discrimination and loss of revenue result. If there is one, as in other areas, some producers' goods will almost inevitably be caught at relatively high rates.

This discussion of indirect taxes is based upon the assumption that they are shifted forward to the consumers of the products. As is well known, there are, without question, exceptions to this rule. With customs duties and flexible exchange rates, the duties may alter the rates, and thus the distribution of the tax burden will be materially altered. These complications of course destroy, in part, the characteristics of the tax as a levy related to consumption and result in greater similarity between the indirect taxes and a haphazardly distributed income tax.

FORMS OF INDIRECT TAXES

Developed economies have a choice of different types of indirect taxes, including customs, excises, and sales taxes of various forms. A relatively underdeveloped economy, however, is much more restricted. Retail sales taxes are out of the question because of the dominance of retail trade by very small establishments, the lack of records, and the lack of literacy on the part of the shopkeepers. When a high percentage of all manufactured goods is imported, there is little to be gained by using a sales tax at a preretail level in place of customs duties, and the latter are much simpler to collect. Thus customs must constitute the primary form of indirect tax, and, on the whole, administering them is simple. However, as domestic production of goods previously reached by customs increases, some use of excises becomes desirable if the same pattern of tax burden is to be retained. If, of course, the primary purpose of the duty is to protect the foreign exchange position, or to provide protection for domestic industry, an equivalent excise is not needed. In the eight African countries, the high-duty goods of which domestic production has greatly increased are liquor and tobacco products, and for the most part steep excises have been introduced. There are some exceptions, as in Ghana, where the elimination of low-quality illicit production was regarded as more important initially than tax revenue. High taxation of these items is presumed to be less dangerous for incentives than similar taxation of general luxury items. Excessive rates, however, may check development of the industries, which may offer important secondary benefits to the economy.

All developing economies that rely heavily on customs must look forward to the future, when, with foreign trade constituting a constantly declining portion of national income, other tax resources must be developed. A universal trend in tax systems has been the forced movement away from customs duties as domestic production rises.

THE SPECIAL CASE OF MOTOR FUEL TAXATION

One characteristic of most developing economies is the great emphasis on road transport; while railways are important in some African countries and rail lines are being extended, the new economies are primarily dependent upon motor transport, and the use of both cars and trucks has grown rapidly. The commercial principle of highway finance has particular merit under such circumstances, although, because of indirect benefits, some support of road construction from other revenues may be justified. The levying of taxes on motor fuel for road building not only will facilitate attainment of optimum allocation of resources between road and rail transport, but also will lessen the pressure on income taxes and other levies which have potential adverse effects on the economy.

THE QUESTION OF TARIFF PROTECTION

Distinct from the use of tariffs as a source of revenue is their employment for protection of new industry. The infant-industry argument for tariffs has particular attraction and considerable merit in underdeveloped economies. The tariffs are, of course, unnecessary if from the stage of initial production the country has such significant comparative advantages that the producers can outsell those of other countries. Rhodesian cigarette production appears to be a good example. But frequently this is not the case. Although new industry will offer very significant secondary benefits to the economy, there is no comparative advantage except cheap labor, and during the early years of expansion the industry cannot compete with well-established large-volume foreign firms. Even if the country has not, and in the foreseeable future will not, have comparative advantage along any industrial lines, it may still be economically justified in protecting industry, because of the secondary benefits and the assurance that profits from the exporting industry will go to home products, the foreign exchange from the exports being used to buy producers' goods instead of consumption goods. But even if the program cannot be justified economically, many newly developing countries regard industrialization as such an important goal in itself as to warrant protection. There are, of course, obvious limitations to the policy; the higher cost of living and the possibly inferior goods could conceivably check incentives, just as revenue tariffs do. But the gains from the program are frequently regarded as sufficient to overcome these considerations.

Of the eight African countries, Rhodesia has made the greatest use of protection and has been relatively successful in bringing industrial development, although some experts in that country question the over-all effectiveness of the program. The East African countries have also made substantial use of protective tariffs, primarily because of the pressure from Kenya, which has thus far had the greatest potentials. The policy has been under fire from Uganda and Tanganyika, which have argued that their consumers have borne much of the cost while Kenya has experienced most of the gain. In Ghana and Nigeria, only limited protection is being given, and the tariffs are still designed primarily for revenue purposes.

A related question is that of exemption from customs duties for materials, supplies, and equipment for new industries. This may be handled on a firm-by-firm basis similar to the pioneer companies legislation, as is done in West Africa, or on a general industry-wide basis, as in East Africa. The need for such action usually arises because some industrial goods are deliberately taxed, others are reached by the catchall category, often at fairly high rates, and some goods are used for both production and consumption purposes. Again, the firm-by-firm approach can cause the same type of delay as the income tax concession; while it has greater potentialities for exact planning, it is inferior in general to the broader industry approach of East and Central Africa. Frequently in either case, for administrative reasons, it is easier to grant the firms refunds of duties paid rather than to exempt them from paying duty, if items of the same classes are to remain taxable to other users.

EXPORT DUTIES

A characteristic feature of many underdeveloped countries is the export of basic materials, such as farm products or ore, often primarily of one or a few commodities. Exports are frequently channeled through a governmental or semigovernmental marketing board. Under such circumstances, governments typically levy export duties, either as a fixed amount per physical unit or related to price. The effect, at given exchange rates, is to reduce the net income of the producers of the basic products. Such duties have several advantages. World prices of these basic products often fluctuate substantially; in good years the governments can obtain large sums of tax revenue for use in economic development and, at the same time, cushion the economy from the inflationary effects of the sharp rise in incomes of the producers not accompanied by an increase in domestic output of consumption goods. Since the base of the levies is physical output or gross price, it is argued that they have less effect in restricting production than would income taxes imposed upon the net earnings. Administration is very simple so long as marketing boards are used.

On the other hand, there are major objections to this form of tax. The primary one, as stressed by P. T. Bauer,[4] is that such taxes, since they are directly related to output and apply to all producers, small and large, do have serious adverse effects in reducing output of the products and thus retard economic growth. The typical income tax applies only to the higher-income groups; the export duties hit the small producer on the margin between subsistence and market farming. To many students of the question, this consideration is so important as to outweigh all others. The taxes are also discriminatory against the producers of those crops subject to tax, and inevitably there will be some shifting of resources from these crops to others, or to greater production for the domestic market. From an equity standpoint, it is difficult to justify the imposition of particularly heavy taxes on the producers of certain goods and not on others. It should also be noted that revenues are highly unstable.

Of the eight African countries, the three in West Africa, plus Uganda and Zanzibar, gain a significant share of revenue from export duties. While these taxes have fluctuated sharply in yield, they have been highly productive of revenue. It is difficult to ascertain any actual effects in discouraging production, but the taxes have been subjected to this criticism. Kenya, Tanganyika, and Rhodesia have deliberately avoided any significant use of export duties because of fear of the dangers for the maintenance of market production.

TAXATION OF LAND AND OTHER PROPERTY

Of all forms of taxation, that on land offers the least danger to economic development per dollar of revenue obtained. Moreover, taxation of other forms of property is potentially less dangerous than forms whose impact is initially on income or immediate uses of income. Rapid economic growth, with its accompanying expansion

[4] See P. T. Bauer and B. S. Yamey, *The Economics of Underdeveloped Countries* (Chicago: University of Chicago Press, 1957).

of metropolitan areas, brings sharp increases in land values, which reflect economic rent. This is a surplus return unnecessary to make factor supplies available for use. Taxation of these rapidly increasing land values will have no effect upon the development, but will lessen the burden of other taxes and has substantial merit from an equity standpoint in checking the growth of large fortunes from land speculation. Taxation of land differs from taxation of income from land in two ways. First, idle or underutilized land is taxed much more effectively by the former. Second, there is no direct connection between the amount of the land tax to be paid during the year and the income earned. The lump-sum nature of the land tax, once assessed, is an incentive to greater and more efficient production, whereas income taxation or export duties may have the opposite effect.

Moreover, taxation of other property—buildings, motor vehicles, and the like—offers less danger to incentives than levies directly related to the earning and use of income. Application of moderate taxes to buildings in urban areas has added justification on the benefit principle, since the construction of the buildings is directly responsible for additional municipal services.

Unfortunately, however, in many underdeveloped areas of the character of the eight African countries, there are serious limitations in the way of effective use of property taxes. In West Africa, and to a considerable extent in the other countries as well, there are no registered land titles, except in a few cities, and essentially no private ownership, execpt of some urban land. In some areas, even, for example, in Ghana, there is still a substantial amount of nomadic agriculture, with persons moving on to a new site in the jungle as the present plot loses fertility. Even in many cities, such as Accra, there are no cadastral surveys or title registry, or clear titles of ownership. As a consequence of these conditions, there is no taxation of rural land at all (with the exception of a low rate tax on some farm land in Uganda). Urban property taxation is confined to improvements in the Ghanaian cities and to annual rental value (with no taxation of unimproved land) in Lagos and a few other Nigerian cities. In Kenya and Tanganyika, however, where urban land titles are clearly defined, there is taxation of land values in the urban areas, with improvements free of tax. In Uganda and Rhodesia, both land and improvements are taxed, but the former at a much higher rate. In the rural areas the occupiers do not pay rent for the use of the land.

While the African countries do not have the large land holdings problem characteristic of some underdeveloped countries, the general field of land taxation offers perhaps the greatest opportunity for improvements in their tax structures. However, before this can be accomplished, registry of rights of ownership or use of land and land surveys are required. Since in many instances there are no land sales, figures of land values must be built up through classification of land by use, fertility, etc., and ascertainment of potential income. If farm product prices fluctuate sharply or substantial inflation occurs, a workable system for revision of land values is imperative, or the relative contribution of the land tax to over-all revenues will not be maintained. When the land is not owned by the individual, but the latter has occupancy rights, the levy may technically be called a rent, but the effect will be exactly the same as if it is designated as a tax.

CONCLUSION

The tax system has four major functions in an underdeveloped economy seeking a rapid rate of growth: curtailment of consumption of above-subsistence families; curtailment of use of resources for capital formation regarded as of little value to economic development; provision of funds to the government to facilitate transfer of the freed resources; and the provision of incentives to alter economic activity in a fashion favorable to economic growth. The tax system must be designed in such a way as to fulfill these functions with a minimum of adverse incentive effects. The means and potentialities for accomplishing these goals have been reviewed in the light of the experience of eight countries of tropical Africa.

An income tax offers much less potentiality than it does in a mature economy, partly for administrative reasons and partly because of the greater dangers of adverse incentive effects. It must, in its usual form, be confined to a small percentage of the population and must have a simpler structure than in mature economies, with allowances being adjusted in terms of the circumstances of the economies (e.g., extended families). However, an income tax properly conceived for the conditions can yield considerable revenue with little danger; it is also the most satisfactory way to reach speculative and other gains arising from rapid growth and is a form of tax that will automatically grow in relative importance as the economy expands.

While the income tax, as such, is not suitable as a mass tax in such economies, African experience suggests that a variant of it, the personal tax, a simple graduated tax applied to all income earners, can implement the need for some form of mass direct tax with little danger to the economy. This levy encourages persons to move from the subsistence economy to the market economy rather than vice versa.

Corporate taxes, while in themselves having little effect in freeing resources for government, will provide substantial funds and check the flow of profits outside the country. Potential adverse economic effects can be lessened by liberal loss carry-forward provisions and accelerated depreciation rules. African experience suggests that these general concessions are far more satisfactory than tax-holiday concessions to particular firms. Depreciation allowances may be adjusted in such a way as to aid the channeling of capital formation into desired lines.

In theory, an expenditure tax would be superior to an income tax in a developing economy by offering incentive to save, and having less danger of adverse effects on other incentives. In fact, the difference is not likely to be great under conditions in which the primary incentive for economic advancement is increased consumption. Furthermore, such a tax is even less feasible for administration than the income tax, even if limited to a relatively small high-income group.

Indirect taxation, primarily in the form of customs duties, offers potentialities for additional revenue beyond the amounts that can feasibly be collected from direct taxes, in large measure because of administrative considerations. Like the expenditure tax, the duties offer potential incentive advantages over the income tax, but the effects on the utility of income, given the circumstances of an under-developed economy, are likely to negate most of these advantages. There is particular danger that very sharp increases in indirect taxes on luxury goods will affect morale, which is significant for economic growth. Export duties are particularly attractive to countries concentrating on the export of one or a few items, since large sums of revenue can be obtained in good years at little administrative cost. However, the potential adverse effects on production are likely to be worse than those of income taxation. Of all forms of taxes, those on land offer the greatest potentialities for expansion with a minimum of adverse effects, but their use is restricted severely by the landownership and title registry situations in many underdeveloped countries.

SELECTED REFERENCES

Bibliography on Taxation in Underdeveloped Countries. Cambridge: Harvard Law School, 1962. A very detailed bibliography, by individual country.

Chelliah, R. J., *Fiscal Policy in Underdeveloped Countries.* London: George Allen and Unwin, 1960. Primary reference to India.

Goode, R., "Taxation of Saving and Consumption in Underdeveloped Countries." *National Tax Journal,* Vol. XIV (December, 1961), pp. 305–322.

Hicks, U. K., *et al., Federalism and Economic Growth in Underdeveloped Countries.* London: George Allen and Unwin, 1961. A symposium.

Heller, J., and K. M. Kauffman, *Tax Incentives for Industry in Less Developed Countries*. Cambridge: Harvard Law School, 1963.

Prest, A. R., *Public Finance in Underdeveloped Countries*. London: Weidenfeld and Nicolson, 1962. One of the best general analyses of the question.

Taxes and Fiscal Policy in Underdeveloped Areas. New York: United Nations Technical Assistance Administration, 1954.

Van Philips, Paul A. M., *Public Finance and Less Developed Economy*. The Hague: Martinus Nijhoff, 1957. Primary reference to Latin America.

Index

Accelerated depreciation, 35–36, 152–153
Accra
  personal taxes in, 64, 65, 77, 79–80
  property taxes in, 103–106
Administration
  of customs duties, 91–95
  of excises, 96–97
  of income taxes, 51–59
  of personal taxes, 71–80
  problems of, 147
Administrative staffs, 51–54
Ad valorem tariffs, 87
Africanization, of income tax staffs, 52–53
Agriculture, and economic development, 16
Allocation of taxing powers
  in East Africa, 133–139
  in Nigeria, 128–131
  in Rhodesia, 122–123
  in Uganda, 139–140
Allowances
  depreciation, 35–36, 152–153
  initial, 34–35, 152–153
  investment, 35–36, 152–153
  personal, 36–37
Andic, F., 60
Appraisal, for customs duties, 92–93
Assessment
  committees for, for personal taxes, 74–76

under income taxes, 54
for property taxes, 103–116
Averaging of income, 47

Badenoch, A. C., 75
Balance-of-payments problems, 85, 99–101, 157
Barber, W. J., 24
Bauer, P. T., 161
British traditions, 8–9
Buganda, 9, 10, 75–77, 139–140
Bulawayo, property tax in, 115–117
Bunyoro, 10
Business expenses
  for income tax, 35–36
  for personal tax, 75

Capital allowances, see Depreciation allowances
Capital gains, 33, 150
Capital intensity, 16
Carry-over of losses, 36, 162
Catchall categories, in tariffs, 89–90
Cess, 118
Chelliah, R. J., 162
Children, income tax allowances for, 36–37
Cigarettes
  customs duties on, 87
  excise taxes on, 95–97
Civil service, status of, 8–9
Cloves, 6, 99

Coleman, J. C., 23
Collection
  of customs duties, 93–94
  of income tax, 55
  of personal tax, 77–79
Colonial Model Income Tax Ordinance, 32
Commonwealth preference, 86, 93
Company taxes, *see* Corporation income taxes
Concessions for new industry
  under customs duties, 86
  under income taxes, 34–35, 152–155
Consolidated allowance system, 36
Coordination, of economic development, 16–21
Corporation income taxes
  depreciation deductions under, 35–36, 152–153
  rates of, 47–49
  relative reliance on, 27
  significance of, for economic development, 151–155
  structure of, 47–49
  tax concessions under, for new industry, 34–35, 152–155
Coverage
  of income taxes, 48–49
  of personal taxes, 79–81
Cox-George, N. A., 82
Credits
  for dependents, 36–37
  tax, Rhodesia, 39
Crown land, 106–108
Cultural features, and economic development, 8, 12–13
Currency systems, 2
Customs duties
  and economic development, 156–160
  for protection, 84–85
  rates of, 87–90
  relative reliance on, 83–84
  sharing of revenue from, Nigeria, 129
  structure of, 84–90
Customs procedures, 91–95

Data-processing equipment, 57–58
Democracy, 8
Dependents, deductions for, 36–37
Depreciation allowances, 35–36, 152–153
Direct taxes, relative reliance on, 26–27
Dissolution, of the Federation of Rhodesia and Nyasaland, 126

Distributable pool
  in East Africa, 138–139, 142–143
  in Nigeria, 128, 142–143
Dividends, income tax treatment of, 33–34
Double taxation of dividend income, 33–34, 152
Dual economies, 20–22

East Africa
  Commission of Inquiry on Income Tax, 59
  Common Services Organization, 30, 32, 94, 134–135
  company tax in, 47–49
  customs duties in, 83–93
  description of, 5–6, 133–134
  excise taxes in, 95–97
  financing of federal elements in, 30, 133–139
  High Commission, 32, 135
  income taxation in, 31–60
  tax concessions to aid new industry in, 35–36, 152–153
  see also Kenya, Tanganyika, Uganda, Zanzibar
Eastern Nigeria
  description of, 127
  income taxation in, 31–59
  personal taxes in, 63
  property taxes in, 106–108
Economic development
  goal of, 144–145
  relation of tax policies to, 144–165
  tax concessions to aid, 35–36, 152–156
EDP equipment, 57–58
Education, need for, 14–16
Educational expenses, income tax allowances for, 38
Educational requirements, of income tax staff, 52–53
Effectiveness
  of customs enforcement, 93–94
  of income tax enforcement, 56–57
  of personal tax enforcement, 79–80
Enforcement
  of customs duties, 93–94
  of excises, 96–97
  of income taxes, 55–57
  of personal taxes, 79–80
Excise taxes
  and economic development, 158–159
  relative reliance on, 84
  structures of, 95–97
Exempt income, income tax, 34

Exemptions
  under income taxes, 36–37
  under personal taxes, 76–77
Expenditure tax, 157
Export duties
  and economic development, 160–161
  relative reliance on, 84
  structure of, 97–99
Extended family system, 13, 36–37, 150

Federalism, fiscal aspects of
  in East Africa, 133–139
  general review of, 29–30
  in Nigeria, 127–132
  in Rhodesia and Nyasaland, 119–126
  in Uganda, 139–149
Federation
  elements of, in East Africa, 30, 32, 94, 134–135
  future of, in Rhodesia, 126
Federation of Rhodesia and Nyasaland, see Rhodesia
Flat-rate personal taxes, 64–65
Foreign exchange problem, 85, 157
Foreign income, 33
Foreign trade, 19
Freetown, property tax in, 109
Fulani, 13, 151

Ghana
  company tax in, 47–49
  customs duties in, 83–95
  description of, 2–3
  excise taxation in, 95–97
  export duties in, 97–99
  income tax in, 31–60
  PAYE in, 43
  personal tax in, 61–82
  property tax in, 103–106
  purchase tax in, 99–101
  socialism in, 18–19
  tax concessions to industry in, 153–155
Goode, R., 162
Government enterprise, 18
Graduated personal taxes, 65–82
Gross Domestic Product, taxes as percentage of, 25–36

Heller, J., 155, 165
Hicks, U. K., 24, 82, 118, 162
Hut taxes, 62

Incentive effects
  of customs duties, 157
  of export duties, 161

of income taxes, 148
of personal taxes, 151
Income, ascertainment of, for personal taxes, 74–76
Income rate, Lagos, 42–43
Income tax, company, see Corporation income taxes
Income Tax Management Act
  in East Africa, 135
  in Nigeria, 130–131
Income tax, personal
  allowances for dependents under, 36–37
  deductions for, 35–39
  and economic development, 147–150
  incentive effects of, 148
  PAYE under, 43–46
  procedure under, 54–59
  rates of, 39–43
  relation of, to personal tax, 63
  relative burdens of, 43–45
  relative reliance on, 26–27
  staffs for, 51–54
  structure of, 31–50
  taxable income under, 33–34
  withholding under, 43–46
Independence, dates of, 3
Indians, in East Africa, 11, 56, 134
Indirect taxes
  and economic development, 155–160
  incentive effects of, 157
  relative reliance on, 26–27
  structure of, 83–101
Industry
  need for, 16
  tax concessions for, 86, 152–155
Inflexibility, of territorial tax revenues, 124–125
Infrastructure, 18
Ingham, K., 24
Initial allowances, 35–36
Insurance premiums, income tax allowance for, 38
International Bank for Reconstruction and Development, 14, 23, 24
Investment allowances, 35–36
Irregular income, 47

Jangali, 64, 151

Kaldor, N., 19, 85, 105, 157
Kampala, property taxes in, 109–110
Kauffman, K. M., 155, 165
Kenya
  description of, 5–7, 21
  dual economy in, 21–22

Kenya, Fiscal Commission in, 140, 143
  local taxes in, 64, 110–113
  personal taxes in, 61–82
  property taxes in, 110–113
  white settlers in, 11
  see also East Africa
Kimble, G. H. T., 24

Lagos
  income rate in, 42–43, 50, 55
  income tax in, 32, 36–46, 50
  personal tax in, 61–82
  property tax in, 12, 107
Land
  ownership of, 12, 103
  taxation of, 102–118, 161–162
  title situation, 103, 109
Lebanese merchants, 11
Liquor
  customs duties on, 87
  excise taxes on, 95–97
Local governments
  use of personal taxes by, 62–63
  use of property taxes by, 102–118
Local tax structures, 29
Loss carry-over, under income tax, 36, 162
Lugard, Lord, 62, 107
Lund, F., 118
Lusaka, 115
Luxury basis for customs duties, 87–88
Luxury consumption, and tax policy, 156–157

Manifest, 91
Married persons, tax treatment of
  under income taxes, 36–37
  under personal taxes, 70–71
Masai, 13
Mau Mau, 6, 21
Medical expenses, deduction of, for income tax, 39
Minimum income tax payments, 42–43
Monckton Commission, 125–126
Motor fuel taxation, 159
Murray, J. F. N., 104, 118

Nairobi, site value taxation in, 110–112
Nationalism, and economic development, 10–11
Nigeria
  company tax in, 47–49
  customs duties in, 83–95
  description of, 2, 10, 127
  excise taxes in, 95–97
  export duties in, 98

financing federalism in, 30, 127–133
income taxes in, 31–60
PAYE in, 43–44
personal taxes in, 61–82
property taxes in, 108–109
tax concessions to industry in, 153–154
Northern Nigeria
  description of, 127–128
  income taxes in, 31–60
  personal taxes in, 61–82
  property taxes in, 106–108
Northern Rhodesia
  description of, 6, 120
  income tax surcharges in, 42, 122
  personal taxes in, 61–82
  property taxes in, 114–115
Nyasaland
  description of, 6, 120
  personal taxes in, 61–82
  property taxes in, 114
Nyerere, Julius, 5, 139

Operation, of customs systems, 91–95
Orewa, G. Oka, 59, 82
Origin rule, 141–142
Owner-occupied homes, income tax treatment of, 33

PAYE, 43–46, 70
Perry, J. H., 154
Personal allowances, under income taxes, 36–37
Personal income taxes, see Income tax, personal
Personal taxes
  assessment of, 74–76
  collection of, 77–79
  and economic development, 150–151
  economic effects of, 150–151
  effectiveness of, 79–80
  enforcement of, 78–79
  exemptions from, 76–77
  nature of, 61–62
  PAYE with, 70
  procedure of, 71–80
  rates of, 64–69
  relation of, to income taxes, 63
  relative reliance on, 63–64
Personnel
  for customs administration, 94–95
  selection and training of, for income tax administration, 51–53
  shortage of trained, 14–15
Phoenix Group, 143
Pioneer companies tax relief, 153–155
Poll taxes, 61–65

Population, of the countries, 3
Population-resources relationship, 7–8
Preferential tariffs, 93
Prest, A. R., 165
Presumptive income, 34–35
Private companies, income tax treatment of, 47–49
Procedure
  for customs duties, 91–95
  for income taxes, 54–58
  for personal taxes, 71–82
Progression
  in income tax rates, 39–42
  in personal tax rates, 65–70
Property taxation, 102–118, 161–162
Protection, tariffs for, 84–86, 159–160
Purchase tax, in Ghana, 99–101

Race prejudices, 11
Raisman, Sir Jeremy, 121–122, 128–129, 137–138
Rate determination, personal tax, 72
Rate structures, of tariffs, 86–90
Rates
  of company taxes, 47
  of customs duties, 86–90
  of excise taxes, 94–97
  of export duties, 97–99
  of personal income taxes, 39–43
  property, see Property taxation
  of property taxes, 107–109, 111–115
  of tariffs, 86–90
Relative burdens
  of personal income taxes, 44
  of total tax levels, relative to national product, 23–24
Relatives, allowances for, 28
Rental basis, for property taxation, 104, 106–108, 117
Rental value, of owner-occupied homes, 33
Reproduction cost basis for property taxation, 103–106
Resources, relative to population, 7–8
Retail sales taxes, 123, 158
Returns
  for income tax, 46–47
  for personal tax, 73–74
Revenue importance
  of company taxes, 27
  of customs duties, 28, 83–84
  of excises, 28
  of export duties, 26
  of personal income taxes, 27
  of personal taxes, 27, 63–64
Revenue structures, summary of, 25–30

Rhodesia (Federation of Rhodesia and Nyasaland)
  company taxes in, 47–48
  customs duties in, 47–49, 83–95, 160
  description of, 6, 120–121
  dual economies, 21–22
  excise taxes in, 95–97
  financing federalism in, 30, 120–126
  future of, 126
  heavy reliance on income tax in, 26–27
  income taxes in, 31–60
  personal taxes in, 61–82
  property taxes in, 114–116
  surcharge system in, 42, 122
  see also Northern Rhodesia, Nyasaland, Southern Rhodesia
Roadblocks, for tax collection, 78
Rockefeller Brothers Fund, 59

Salary scales, for income tax staffs, 51–52
Sales taxes, role of, in developing economies, 123, 158
Selwyn, P., 24
Sierra Leone
  company taxes in, 47–49
  customs duties in, 83–95
  description of, 2–4
  excise taxes in, 95–97
  export duties in, 98
  income taxes in, 31–60
  personal taxes in, 61–82
  property taxes in, 109
Simplification, of income taxation, 36, 58–59, 148–149
Site value basis of property taxation, 109–116
Smith, A. H., 153
Smuggling, 93–94
Southern Rhodesia
  description of, 6, 22, 120
  income tax surcharges in, 42, 122
  PAYE in, 46, 71
  personal taxes in, 61–82
  property taxes in, 115–116
Supplements, to wages and salaries, 33
Surcharges, territorial, to Federation income tax, 42, 122

Tanganyika
  description of, 133–134
  local taxes in, 64, 113–114
  personal taxes in, 61–82
  property taxes in, 113–114
  see also East Africa
Tariffs
  importance of, 83–84
  policy on, 85–86

Tariffs, procedures for, 91–95
    for protection, 84–86, 159–160
    role of, in developing economies, 156–160
    structures of, 84–90
Tax coordination, in East Africa, 30, 32, 85, 134–136
Tax credit system, in Rhodesia, 39
Tax holiday, 153–155
Tax policy
    disagreements over, in East Africa, 134–136
    and economic development, 145–165
Tax rates
    of income taxes, 39–42
    of personal taxes, 64–69
    of property taxes, 107–109, 111, 112–115
Tax returns
    for income tax, 46–47
    for personal tax, 73–74
Tax structures, summary of, 25–29
Taxable income, 33–34
Taxpayer rolls
    income tax, 54
    personal tax, 72–73
    property tax, 105, 107
Taxpayers, number of
    income taxes, 48–49
    personal taxes, 79–81
Timing, of income tax payments, 46–47
Townships, in Nigeria, 108
Training programs, for income tax staffs, 53
Tress, R. C., 128
Tribalism, and economic development, 9, 10

Uganda
    description of, 5, 10, 133–134
    export duties in, 99
    federal elements in, 139–140

personal taxes in, 61–81
property taxes in, 109–110
see also East Africa
Undistributed profits problem, 48–49
United Kingdom, source of income tax personnel, 52–53
United Nations, 104, 108, 165

Valuation, for property tax purposes
    in Ghana, 103–106
    in Kenya, 110–113
    in Nigeria, 106–109
    in Northern Rhodesia, 114–115
    in Sierra Leone, 109
    in Southern Rhodesia, 115–116
    in Uganda, 109–110
Van Philips, P., 165

Wald, H. P., 102, 118
Ward, Susan, 24
Watson, T. Y., 24
West Africa, general features of, 2–5, 20
Western Nigeria
    description of, 127
    income taxes in, 31–59
    personal taxes in, 61–82
    property taxes in, 106–108
White settlers
    in Kenya, 11, 12
    in Rhodesia, 12
Withholding, of income taxes, 43–46, 70
Women
    income tax treatment of, 36–37
    personal tax treatment of, 70–71
    role of, in tropical Africa, 12–13

Zanzibar
    customs duties in, 83–95
    description of, 6
    export duties in, 99
    participation of, in East African joint income tax system, 32
    property taxes in, 113